to
Joe,

An ocean away
the shared dreams
still entice.

Jim
Spenly

Rebuilding Rose

The Tale of an Atkin Packet Sloop

Rebuilding Rose

The Tale of an Atkin Packet Sloop

Jim Spaulding

MBI

Dedicated to my better half, Cheryl,
the protector of all things *Rose*.
And to all backyard do-it-yourselfers
trying to save old boats,
may The Force be with you

This edition first published in 2004 by MBI Publishing Company, Galtier Plaza, Suite 200, 380 Jackson Street, St. Paul, MN 55101-3885 USA

The information in this book is true and complete to the best of our knowledge. All recommendations are made without any guarantee on the part of the author or Publisher, who also disclaim any liability incurred in connection with the use of this data or specific details.

We recognize that some words, model names, and designations, for example, mentioned herein are the property of the trademark holder. We use them for identification purposes only. This is not an official publication.

Motorbooks International titles are also available at discounts in bulk quantity for industrial or sales-promotional use. For details write to Special Sales Manager at Motorbooks International Wholesalers & Distributors, Galtier Plaza, Suite 200, 380 Jackson Street, St. Paul, MN 55101-3885 USA.

ISBN 0-7603-1884-0

Designed by Brenda Canales

Printed in the United States

Contents

PREFACE

My wife, Cheryl, and I have been around the Chesapeake Bay since we were children, and we have sailed together since the mid-1960s. In 1997 we were looking for a sailboat, but my empathetic bride bought a pile of old lumber masquerading as a boat. Six years and many tales later, *Rose* is a restored boat. Some of the stories of her restoration were published as "A Story of a *Rose*" in Ira Black's *Nor'Easter Magazine*.

Rose was relaunched in 2001 for commissioning and outfitting, with a shakedown cruise and maiden voyage in 2002, and final finishing in 2003. The project took six years, costing over $15,000 and 5,000 hours of work. The following question did arise: Why blow years working on a boat when we could be using one?

By the value system of the 1990s, there is no money in it. The boat cost more than an alternative, and my time is worth negative money in resale value. I cannot defend these activities with logic, but I do have some thoughts.

We accomplished something memorable; it was one of the defining moments in our lives. If anyone ever asks who Jim and Cheryl Spaulding were, somehow restoring *Rose* and writing the book are part of the answer. I have pride and confidence that comes from accomplishing something difficult because I kept at it until completion. The pride comes from pulling victory from the jaws of defeat.

Today, there is also an element of simplicity creeping into our madcap world that enables us to examine living in another age and moving at a speed slow enough to appreciate the things around us. Clearly *Rose* provided me with an opportunity for personal growth and a sense of craftsmanship.

There is also the merit in the preservation of a bit of history. *Rose* looks like a classic yacht. Her gaff rig, sheer line, and proud bowsprit all drag our minds back to our shared culture, another age, and our maritime heritage. There is a feeling that we are good people who do good things, like helping those in need and taking in stray dogs.

Rose is the image of what we see as our history. Bob Green, the patriarch of Bay Boat Works said, "Just seeing that boat here makes me smile." A stranger once said, "Can I just look? She makes me feel good."

Sailing her is a kick! There is a touch of whimsy with her dashing appearance, bright colors, wood galore, *Rose* nameplates, white tipped spars, and controversial electric drive. Of course, there is the practical aspect of knowing firsthand *everything* there is to know about the vessel. That kind of confidence is the result of the intimacy that only a builder can have. An old adage says, "What I hear I forget. What I see I remember. What I do I understand." Maybe I can even pass on some of what I learned in the how-to sections aided by drawings and graphs. However, lest I bore you, most of the technical sections use a what-to-do approach, leaving *how* to do the job up to you. Ultimately, if we need a simple answer to the question "Why?" I believe we would have to blame it on a bad case of "Woody Disease," as you might glean from the following letter.

I hope this book will be helpful, encouraging, and maybe even a little endearing. I hope you enjoy it as much as I enjoyed writing it for you. Thank you for joining us on a wonderful voyage!

ACKNOWLEDGMENTS

- Special thanks to Bob and Pam Appleton for starting the writing off
- Thanks to Ira Black at *Nor'Easter Magazine,* who encouraged and assisted in getting these stories and the book published
- Janie Meneely at *Chesapeake Bay Magazine,* who sent me to a publisher
- Janet Spaulding, my editor, agent, whip, and wonderful daughter-in-law
- The team of David and Steven Spaulding & Jennifer and Rob Duff
- Mr. and Mrs. Atkin for their encouragement and information
- Bob Swift and Jeff Carstens for electrical systems that actually do things
- My brother, Tom Spaulding, for solving many problems and for his crucial hands
- Al Kotake, who helped when he knew I didn't have a clue what I was doing
- Frank Pinder, Don Green, Bill, and the great crew at Bay Boat Works
- To Ed at Hillside Machine for the parts you created for *Rose*
- To Mike and others at Haines Restorations, who were there with a smile
- To George Hazard, my ship's carpenter and mentor in the Dark Days
- Meade and Cheryl Breese, for making the breezes more useful
- My neighbors, for tolerating weekends and late-night noises and spotlights
- Students, friends, and business colleagues, for listening to my babblings
- To Jack and Susie for personal harassment at critical times
- Thanks to the many folks who encouraged us while we worked on *Rose,* the articles, and the book
- To the readers who greet us on the Bay with "Hey, *Rose.*" We love you!
- Most of all, thanks to MBI Publishing Company for a fine job

A LETTER FROM A FRIEND

Woody Disease: A condition characterized by obsessive-compulsive behavior involving the building and/or restoration of wood vessels. A widely recognized contagion with thousands of infected amateurs who work without pay to build, save, and restore wood boats in boatyards and backyards.

Dear Jim,

I'm sorry to hear of your affliction with the dreaded "Woody Disease," though it's not a surprise, considering the risk of infection at Bay Boat Works due to its colony of wood boats and infected people. I guessed as much from the otherworldly look in your eyes, the smiling, haggard look on your face, and the strong drink and cigar—even before reading this enthusiastic account of your newfound passion.

Most of us with this disease recognize the symptoms once we get into the third stage, and you are already exhibiting classic signs of this highly contagious affliction. I assure you that the haggard appearance and loss of weight is quite usual in the early stages, probably due to overwork and missed mealtimes. There are few credible scientific studies, but some believe that weight loss is accelerated by the ingestion of large amounts of sawdust, which increases fiber in the diet.

You may have already discovered that alcohol helps diminish the pains from repetitive muscle and joint injuries incurred while crawling and working in unusual postures. Cigars help to camouflage sinuses impacted by fine paint particles and sanding dust; the cigars also help to explain the red, swollen eyes.

The widely recognized symptoms of loud speech and wildly articulating gestures may help to communicate while in pain, but hearing loss due to power equipment may also be a contributor to this phenomenon. This is usually a temporary concern since the sufferer rarely cares whether anyone is listening by the time the third stage sets in.

Those with the disease define themselves in terms of our project's size, design, and cost. They rarely identify themselves as an entity separate from the project and usually introduce themselves as "I'm working on the 42-footer, the *Ugly Duckling*, over by dock E."

Psychological symptoms of megalomania and hallucinations center around the project, populated with beliefs that the infected soul can save any vessel, no matter how far gone it may be. The diseased individual dreams of keeping alive traditions that were dead long before they were born. Many dream of huge vessels that deserve to be saved and restored to a beauty they never had in their first few lives. Unfortunately, out of politeness, friends, relatives, and bystanders who get roped into listening to such ravings often smile and placate without confronting the delusions. As a result, some sufferers don't even realize they have the disease at the earliest stages.

The second stage of the disease is the most easily recognized since the effects become more public and the diseased individual may become a social pariah to friends and associates. The good news is that the obsessive-compulsive behavior focuses exclusively on the project at hand. The bad news is that the individual takes on the characteristics of a biblical prophet and recklessly drags friends and relatives into the project as if it were a crusade to save the world. Victims accept virtual martyrdom as weather, insects, and power tools create the most perverse conditions imaginable.

In Tom Sawyer fashion, some visitors may pick up a tool to see what such obviously rewarding work is like. They often leave shortly thereafter, affirming that such labors will give you much needed exercise, but you already look thinner and in better shape. I highlight these items for you since experienced and watchful "Woodys" (those afflicted with the disease) can help distract the victim from disenfranchising loved ones.

Secondary effects may be ignored in the press, but popular wisdom confirms overused credit cards and home equity loans. Credible reports talk of spouses discovering hidden receipts and tools surreptitiously swapped between sufferers to minimize the public recognition of the severity of the disease. Be careful hiding receipts and borrowed tools.

The third stage is less disruptive because the diseased individual, family, and friends integrate the condition into new lifestyles, often with new friends, who also suffer from the disease. By then the first project boat has left the ICU (Intensive Care Unit) stage, and the boat may be classified as "critical but stable." The same might be said of the victim. Friends may still ignore hints of work to be done, but they may visit more because they are hoping that with the end of the project in sight you might return to normal sometime soon.

Often, justification for the ongoing behavior is the pitiful logic that so much effort and money had been invested that the project *must* be finished. The disease is surprisingly long-lived, though symptoms may grow and wane. Remissions have been reported, but sufferers may pass into apparent remission for months, only to be found engulfed in a fresh episode with little warning.

The good news is that survivors can be found in groups such as WANT-MORE (Woodys Anonymous: Not Terribly Motivated Or in Remission Entirely) and WOODYS (WOOdys DYsfunctional Survivors). These groups are pressing the American Medical Association to certify the disease so more research can be done. Perhaps in the future, some cure may even be discovered. In the meantime, we learn to help each other.

And that brings me to friendships. Woodys make great friends! You can depend on me as long as the ice chest is full of beverages and snacks. However, I refuse to pick up tools heavier than 2 pounds for any purpose other than to pass it to you.

Your friend,

Katz
A fellow sufferer

1

A THORNY
LOVE AFFAIR

A rose is a rose is a rose,
unless it's a 6,000-pound
pile of 40-year-old lumber
masquerading as a boat.

I'm blessed with a frugal wife who has a bad buying habit. Cheryl is a sympathy buyer; she feels sorry for things and then buys them. I learned about this quirk when we purchased our first Christmas tree. We returned to our apartment with a 3-foot, two-stalked mass of vegetation with broken branches and few needles.

My blushingly pregnant wife was worried that it was so ugly, nobody would want to take it home, so "it would not have Christmas, even though it gave its life to be a Christmas tree." It took hours of tying greenery to it, so it resembled a tree, before we could decorate it. Thirty years later, in the same spirit, she saved a boat. We longed to sail on a sea-worthy, inexpensive, and easy-to-maintain weekender. She dashed in to save an abandoned wood boat with broken ribs, rotted decks, and rusted hardware because the marina was planning to burn it.

This nightmarish apparition would be perfect, my enthusiastic spouse pointed out, "Just pay the yard fees . . . buy some parts . . . well, maybe a lot of parts . . . a bit of work . . . well, maybe a lot of work . . . but we won't rush, and we can do it *together!*" (The ultimate weapon in any discussion.)

As we stood in the boatyard, she described the curves, solid lines, majestic bowsprit, the wonders of a gaff rig, the smell and feel of wood, and the pride we would feel when we sailed into harbor—but I was not convinced. My experience made it unlikely I could fulfill her dream. I am gifted with three or four thumbs per hand and a knack to do more damage to myself than to the pieces of wood I victimize. We had sailed many boats, but none with a gaff rig, straight keel, and lots of wood.

Cheryl blew past all objections, and prompted by her enthusiasm, I tried to get into the spirit during lunch. Slowly, a plan emerged: clean up, recaulk, fix up, repaint, and dress it up. It would be approximately a two-year project with a tool shop and help. As we finished our crab sandwiches, I promised to think about it.

Riding home, I learned that *Rose* (Omigod, she already had a name) would be finished with red sails and sail into Baltimore a mere year later, just in time to be our anniversary present. My plan was in shambles and I hadn't even agreed yet.

Cheryl tracked down the designer (Atkin & Company of Darien, Connecticut) and arranged to discuss the boat with Mr. Atkin, a New England legend. He and his son had built a strong reputation for a range of classic designs.

Gaff-Rigged Sloop

*by Atkin & Co., Darien, Con-
Address all inquiries to the*

**Atkin Boat Plans
Box 3005
Noroton, Conn: 06820**

DIMENSIONS: L.O.A. 24 *ft.*9 *in.* L.W.L., SAIL AREA 352 sq *ft*, AUXILIARY POWER 5 *to* 8 *hp Universal.*

THIS ABLE LITTLE packet was recently designed for Mr. and Mrs. Robert H. Blair, Maplewood, New Jersey. Below decks she is laid out to provide cruising comfort for two. The double bunk is forward, with headroom of 5 ft 4 in. An enclosed toilet room with water closet and shelves is abaft the bunk on the port side. Opposite this is 3 ft 4 in. unit are lockers and book shelves. A drop-leaf, fitted to the bulkhead, forms the dining table. The galley, in the after end of the cabin, is furnished with two burner stove, shelves, ice box, work counter, sink and lockers. Headroom under the companionway slide is 6 ft 1 in.

The simple rig includes only a jib stay and two shrouds on each side. This is because the gaff-head main permits a generous sail area without necessitating a tall, multi-stayed mast and its attendent rigging. This low-aspect spread of canvas harmonizes with the clipper bow, the trailboards, the sheer line, and the seagoing ·· of this round bilge auxiliary.

ingle cylinder Universal Fisher-
·elops from 5 to 8 hp at slow
It is installed beneath the cockpit floor and bridge deck. Access is through double doors with an opening of 2 ft 4 in. by 2 ft 6 in. The sloop will do a good 7 mph under power, the designer reports.

Twin gasoline tanks, fitted beneath the cockpit seats, have a total capacity of 40 gallons and fill from the deck. The cockpit is 5 ft 5 in. by 5 ft. The self-draining foot well is 2 ft 4 in. by 2 ft 2 in. The deck edge is capped with a 2 in. high bulwark rail; 1 ft 8 in. decks along the waist give ample foot room.

For a small boat, the construction is on the heavy side. Keel and deadwood are sided and moulded 6 in. yellow pine; stem and stern post sided 4 in. yellow pine; frames and floor timbers are white oak; planking is white cedar ¾ in. thick. Decking is 1¼ in. by 2 in. white pine with caulked and payed seams. Plank shears, cabin sides, bulwark rails, and outside joiner work are of mahogany. Hull fastenings are galvanized.

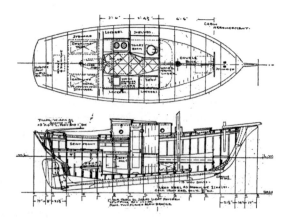

Pequeño's launching announcement from a magazine published in March 1960.

ChiChi, as we found her in 1997 at Bohemia Vista, before she became Rose. The boat-yard was planning to burn her the day after we first saw her.

We spoke with Mr. Atkin and his wife. He reassured me about the sailing characteristics and the stability of the design. We were pleased with a copy of the original plans Mrs. Atkin sent us. She also sent several articles and pictures of the boat launching in 1960. Unfortunately, Mr. Atkin did not live to see his boat restored to its current condition.

The boat was built on Long Island Sound for Mr. and Mrs. Robert H. Blair of Maplewood, New Jersey. The original name was *Pequeño* ("Little One"), but she was referred to as *ChiChi* in the marina. Cheryl tracked down the last owners for us to talk to and assure a clear title.

I was simply outclassed by Cheryl's sales effort. I was left with but one argument: money. I insisted it was too costly and whined, "We can get a fiberglass boat for a few $1,000!"

Cheryl agreed. Confused by her change of tack, I numbly listened as she insisted that we offer only *half* of the $1,400 the boatyard wanted or else she would not let me buy it.

Confused, I took the bait and the boatyard took the offer.

The next day we drove to the marina for a real look at what would become *Rose,* but we were not ready for the reality. The mainsail was torn and discolored; there was corrosion and discoloration everywhere. The ground around it was covered with chips of paint and dried caulk. A screwdriver fit between dried and shrunken planks that had been out of the water for too long. The forward hatch broke off and chunks of the deck crumbled as I tried to tie a line to the bollards. I did a quick survey and was sure the boat was a disaster, so money invested in a professional survey to find more bad news hardly seemed worthwhile. We were the dubious owners of 6,000 pounds of 40-year-old lumber that was masquerading as a boat.

Our "new" boat leaving Bohemia Vista Marina with spars tied to both sides while water, dirt, paint, and caulk fell off with every bump in the road.

It would take at least a year to fix it up, and we could work best in our backyard. I found a mover and waited for the target date. As the tension built, pictures of finished wood capped with glistening white surfaces and highlighted with gleaming brass fittings clouded our brains. It had cost more than the original cost of building a pad and buying stands, blueprints, and books. In days, the dream was buried under a heap of canceled checks and things-to-do lists.

Though the mover was careful, the hull creaked, wobbled, and twisted grotesquely as we shifted her weight from stands to the hydraulic arms of the trailer. Pieces of the rigging and rotten lines gave way as we tied the mast and booms to the rail so we could haul her home. The sounds and appearances were not reassuring, and we almost expected her to fall apart as we traveled over country roads. A day's work of babying her to a flat spot in our backyard ended in a cool drizzle.

After the tired boat mover left, I tried to clean up some of the mess and noticed a hull plank protruding at an odd angle near the keel. I discovered I could stick my hand inside the hull through a gaping hole.

Friends assured us the event was to be expected since the planks had dried out in the boatyard for years, and they were shaken free by transporting. In case you can use my friends' tidbit of wisdom, I'll share it: Wood swells when it gets wet. Wood shrinks when it gets dry. As it changes from one condition to the other, something always goes wrong.

Planks were literally popping off the ribs. The ugly ends protruded into the shadows, streaking the interior with light it had not seen in 40 years. Gobs of goo dripped from her innards like a disemboweled whale.

Apparently, cotton and asphalt had been forced into the spaces between the planks when they were dry. This left no room for the swelling of the wood when it got wet, so the fasteners pulled out as the planks swelled and worked their way loose. Our priority obviously was to stop this trend before the hull collapsed. Long before we planned to, we were forced to strip paint off at least the rib areas so we could refasten the hull planks.

Dismay compounded our exhaustion as we discovered that the purported bottom paint was an amalgam of "stuff" bonded with asphalt. Removal was a problem because the chemicals used for stripping made a mess. A torch or heat gun and a scraper pushed it around with a stench but with little positive effect. Despite ads and gadgets, no technique seemed to work. Dynamite was beginning to look like a viable option.

When I suggested the dynamite alternative, I was met with stony glares from Cheryl, who was becoming the derelict's defender. I learned that maternal instincts do not wilt when the kids leave. Such instincts may be redirected toward worthy recipients, so *Rose* was now protected by a force more powerful than the impregnable layers on her surface. I could see things that were wrong, but as I did the survey to find what was *right,* Cheryl acted as the advocate and defended the boat from accusations.

Days of work with a grinder and sanders revealed usable white cedar planks. As we battled our way through the mess, the good news was that most of the hull planks were not rotted. Cheryl defended each one by pointing them out and saying, "I'm sure you can save this one!" Some wood was in such bad shape, there was not even enough left for screws, but I felt most of the planks could be saved if we could keep them on the ribs. Most of the damage was at the rusted fasteners, through-hull fittings, or where ends butted together. However, as planks joined the rebel contingent going places they didn't belong, it was obvious that all the fasteners below the waterline had to be replaced.

We stripped out a lot of the interior, along with years of debris, to yield proof that roses have thorns; what looked like old wood was rotten wood. The white oak crossbeams and mast step were weak with rot. Apparently, the mast was dropped onto the mast step and cracked the 3-inch thick oak down the middle.

Dismayed, I ripped out the ceilings (strips of wood that line the inside of the hull, beneath the interior and under the berth). Even worse discoveries awaited me. The ribs on both sides of the mast step were rotted out, split, or broken where the planks were popping away. There was little to sit the mast on and nothing left for attaching the planks. Ribs and planks had moved dramatically away from each other with gaps up to an inch between the ribs and the keel. The hull was pulling apart. *Rose* definitely needed professional help.

Safety depended on the integrity of the hull, and after hours of denial I had to accept that we had to rip out and replace, at the very least, five ribs, three crossbeams, and the mast step. Other ribs and crossbeams needed to be sistered or reinforced.

Cheryl noted that this was not *Rose*'s fault. *Rose* was abused in a previous life and I should be more understanding instead of ranting over every little problem. I continued, despite the lambasting.

Crossbeams bolt to the keel and to ribs on either side with heavy-duty 3/8-inch galvanized bolts to pull the crossbeams into slots in the keel. Covered with rust, several twisted in half with little pressure. Cheryl yelled I was "too rough" and that I should "not break any more bolts!" Gentler sampling confirmed my fears; all the bolts in 20 crossbeams were corroded through. They had to be replaced to keep the boat from collapsing under her own weight.

Concerned for the integrity of the hull, I was past reassurance. We cleared room beneath the keel and pulled huge silicon-bronze bolts out, one by one. We then probed the giant beam of the yellow pine keel, the backbone of the vessel. Amazingly, the keel was fine and every keel bolt was in excellent condition. This was our first "not bad news." The keel and most of the wood in the hull was good, just as Mr. Atkin had assured me.

The next question was "What had we missed?" Determined to face the worst, we turned our attention upward. The topsides had degenerated from New England winters and Chesapeake Bay summers. New cabin paint covered coats of older paint and canvas, the trim was in bad shape, and we found a mess when we pulled out the fascia board across the front of the cabin. The king planks were in terrible shape and rot had damaged major components, including the posts on the corner of the cabin.

Once the hull planks were firmly attached, the rest of the stripping and sanding was done and the hull faired to a smoother shape.

Overall, a dozen critical pieces were useless due to rot and damage; 1,000 fasteners and bolts that held it all together could not be saved. Fortunately, most of the wood was okay except where it was damaged by the rusted steel fasteners, bad changes, and poor maintenance. *Rose* was only 37 years old, but she was built on a budget with cheap fasteners and workmanship that guaranteed eventual damage.

We began the survey in a hopeful frame of mind, but as the bad news piled up, it grew harder to maintain perspective. We discovered things we didn't know could be wrong with a boat. Even Cheryl was intimidated by the severity of the problems, so she drove me harder to save her dream. However, each new discovery meant even more work than we first recognized since I knew that wood, once it starts to rot, will not stop just because I plug the leak; the cause must be identified and fixed or the rot will continue. I had no interest in patching it up, only to later have a problem reappear to undermine my work.

Patience was not one of my virtues, and I was now dunked deeply into it. I have since learned that a wood boat is not a project, but an *experience*. During the summer of 1997, I got my first bitter taste of that experience. I tried to take in smaller sips after that. We had just begun, but I could not handle more horrid discoveries.

We had a survey and a task list; now we faced the reality that we had to *rebuild* the boat rather than merely fix it up. Fortunately, Cheryl was looking at the situation through *Rose*-colored glasses and I didn't know how much work rebuilding actually was, so we plugged along, reaffirming that ignorance *is* bliss. Fortunately, the upwelling of hope we all feel in the spring was granted to refresh our souls at exactly the right moment.

The rich greenery of Chester County wrapped around the derelict in the backyard. Tufts of grass and moist earth smoothed the ruts and tire tracks marking her arrival, while the trees blossomed flowers and leaves. Spring had sprung. Cheryl shared her dream with family and friends, and she solicited volunteers. Refreshed by the support of friends and family, we dug in with renewed energy and I took a working vacation to start the restoration.

Little did we know that we would see four springs pass in this lush setting before *Rose* went back to the sea.

I recall a Chinese proverb:
"A trip of a thousand miles starts with but a single step."
However, a certain Indian proverb may have been more appropriate:
"How do you eat an elephant? One bite at a time."

2

REFASTENING A HULL
IS SUCH FUN

The pleasant chirp of birds and bugs was interrupted by my rantings as more planks popped off the ribs. The galvanized steel nails refused to hold planks, but they had no interest in coming out either. It was imperative that we get new bronze screws into the planks ASAP to stem the disintegration. Frantically, we stripped the paint so that we could see to refasten and brace the hull before more planks popped off. Then we realized that the screws were not effective on all the planks. Below the waterline, we had to use nuts and bolts, drawn tight, to force planks into their original relationships with each other.

So began the refastening, before any other work could begin. After a small area around each rib was sanded down to the wood so we could see, each plank was pushed or jacked into position and fastened with screws or bolts. Each screw was a challenge: drill starter hole, countersink the plank, screw into the rib, and hand-tighten without crushing wood or breaking the screw. A through-bolt was a task for two: inside and outside. The outsider drills a counter-sunk hole and runs a bolt through the plank and rib. The insider adds a washer and nut, then hand-tightens them to prevent crushing the wood.

Drill, countersink, screw, hand-tighten. Tell yourself that things look better already. Day after day, we fought planks going places they didn't belong as we coaxed paint and epoxy off surfaces so we could see. Rituals were enhanced with screams or curses before moving to the next item.

Drill, countersink, screw, hand-tighten, slip on junk, and twist left ankle. Another character-building discovery was that wads of cotton, caulking, and asphalt in the spaces between planks had to be removed to pull the planks tightly against the ribs where they belong.

Drill, countersink, screw, hand-tighten, beat on planks until junk falls out of gap, and scrape with a weapon until the plank fits into place.

Drill, countersink, screw became mantra since only a pseudoreligious mindset can assure survival on those hot summer days and nights. The project sounded like a crusade as Cheryl told friends and relatives how "beautiful" *Rose* was and how magnificent she'd be sailing Inner Harbor. They dutifully nodded their heads, smiling uneasily, trying to garner a mental association to the words they heard from the sights confronting them. I admired their patience, as they tried not to say, "But I can see from here through to the other side!"

Drill, countersink, screw, hand-tighten, and coordinate with carpenter George Hazard, who replaced ribs, crossbeams, the mast step, deck planks, and under planks.

Drill, countersink, screw, tighten too far, break another screw. While screwing and bolting hull planks to the ribs, the ends of the planks were bolted to short blocks that splice the ends of two planks together. (The ends of the planks do not join on a rib, but join between the ribs.) Several people were needed to reattach the ends of these planks.

Drill, countersink, screw, then change batteries. At times we screwed extra boards into the plank a few inches from the end and used a clamp to force the two ends together to close the spaces.

Drill, countersink, screw, jack plank in place. As the number of new fasteners passed the 400 mark, my brain obsessed on the idea that *Rose* would be a fine centerpiece for our Fourth of July party. I saw her deck as a launching pad for fireworks, an exciting show for the neighborhood. The festival could end with a stupendous burst of fireworks ignited inside, leading to a suitably enthusiastic bonfire.

Drill, countersink, break screwdriver. Drive the to store for a screwdriver, then buy three as backup. Check out fireworks for sale in the parking lot. Crises of confidence were resolved after politicking by *Rose*'s chief proponent. Streams of visitors appeared, as if by magic, to encourage my labors.

Keel beam and bronze keel bolts were okay, but all else amidships was in trouble. The mast step was so bad, we ripped it out as seen here. Ribs and crossbeams were broken, rotted, and pulled away from the keel, along with a dozen planks around the keel.

Drill, countersink, screw, slice finger, get Band-Aid, and take a break. I suspected the frequent visitors were chartered to snoop around for sources of fire or incendiary materials I might have been harboring for a preemptive strike.

Drill, countersink, screw, hand-tighten, beg friends for help. Harassment of family and friends did elicit assistance and a lot of free supervision.

Drill, countersink, screw, tighten too much, beat plank, feel better. Visitors seemed awed by the scale of the disaster and conditions they encountered. Some wanted to help, but the smart ones simply wanted to escape.

Drill, countersink, screw, slip and gouge wood, add filler to list for later. Slowly the pile of lumber began to resemble the hull of a boat in my mind's eye, if not to the camera, which was unimpressed by my hard work.

Drill, countersink, run bolt in, add washer and nut, hand-tighten. Jack a plank into place amidst chaos and cursing.

In typical Tom Sawyer fashion, some visitors picked up tools to see what such obviously rewarding work felt like. They often left quickly, affirming that such labors gave me much-needed exercise—and they could see I was in better shape already. I assume they used X-ray vision to see through the grinding mask, goggles, gloves, dirt, dust, bruises, scabs, Band-Aids, and swaths of Ace bandages that adorned my body.

Drill, countersink, run bolt in, add washer and nut, hand-tighten, tell myself it's okay. During the refastening process we had to bolt crossbeams to and between opposing ribs, while compressing planks and ribs toward the keel so the gaps would squeeze down to their original size.

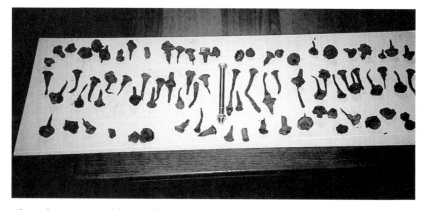

Shown here are rusted hunks of the 80 bolts that held the boat together when it was new. Note the example of what they should be like and that two are not rusted through.

Drill, countersink, run bolt in, add washer and nut, hand-tighten, smack ladder, twist ankle. Call for an ankle brace, while dragging body into shade and begging for a beer. Hope that helpers take over the job. (They use excuses for the unplanned break.) *Rose* narrowly eluded my torch on a daily basis that summer, as my better half maintained a steady flow of visitors and helpers to overcome my reservations and prod me on to grander levels of self-deception.

Drill, countersink, screw, slip and gouge the wood to make more work for later. Throw a temper tantrum and punish the screwdriver. Take a long break, remove the screwdriver from the picnic table where it was embedded up to its shank in redwood.

Drill, countersink, screw, hand-tighten, beg for rain so we can take a break. We still had to deal with the fact that 100 large bolts had to be replaced to keep the boat from falling apart.

Drill, countersink, run bolt, hand-tighten nut, slice finger, get Band-Aid. A major question was how to correct the deformation of the hull. The components had shifted position relative to each other, so even if we screwed the planks to the ribs, it would not have pulled the hull back into its original shape. I researched it, but whatever secret solutions ships' carpenters have for hogging, I couldn't find how to fix it, so I designed my own solution.

Drill, countersink, screw too much, and go right through the wood. Start explaining solution to all the dubious faces around me. Resort to drawings, mockups, demonstrations, and finally more temper tantrums.

Step 1: We braced as many planks as possible to spread the weight over the surface. Then we leveled the deck, since it was most stable, and straightened it relative to the keel. We used the cockpit floor as the flat point for leveling and jacked the boat so it sat exactly as in the design drawing.

Drill, countersink, screw, hand-tighten, swallow filthy wad of asphalt and cotton, beg for glass of any liquid quickly—preferably beer.

We started at the top of the hull and worked down, from front and back to center, to pull the planks tight. Work often went late into the night with halogen lights and sleepy neighbors whose tolerance had worn thin.

Step 2: We started at the bow, stern, and deck edges, working our way down and to the center of the keel, while tightening and refastening as we went.

Drill, countersink, screw, smash knuckles hard, get Band-Aids, hide.

Step 3: As the outer edges firmed up, we jacked the bow and stern to the right heights with the cockpit sole level. This restored the side profile of the boat to design specs.

Drill, countersink, screw, work toward keel. Cheryl avoids the explanation; she claims it hurts her head.

Drill, countersink, run bolt in, add washer and nut, hand-tighten, slice finger on the same edge, get another Band-Aid.

Step 4: The process used a dozen 6-foot stainless straps, 1x3/4 inch attached at the amidships ribs and through-bolted to the sides of the hull about 3 feet from the keel.

Drill, countersink, run bolt in, add washer and nut, hand-tighten too much, break off bolt.

Begin working on the last section of planks closest to the keel. All work like this is done upside down with dirt falling directly into the eyes and mouth.

Step 5: As we tightened and refastened ribs and planks from the top down, and from the ends toward the center, the straps were pulled down to bring the hull and planks together. This action forced the ribs and planks into alignment with the keel.

Drill, countersink, screw, rip fingernail. Grab beer and Band-Aid.

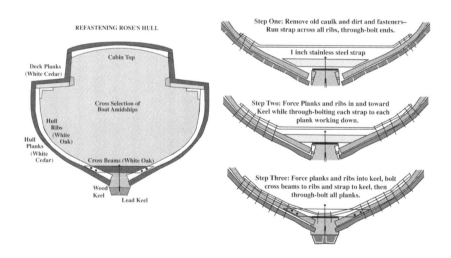

Step 6: Stainless straps pulled ribs to the keel, to bolt to crossbeams. This was scary when the cheap, stainless bolts broke while tightening the nuts. Expensive replacements suggested that you get what you pay for and also reinforced my paranoia about *Rose.*

Drill, countersink, break countersink. Drive to store for new one and get lost for hours. Return with bottle of wine, feeling much better, but forgot to buy replacement countersink.

Drill, countersink, screw, hand-tighten. Buy more screws and bolts. In a morbid moment, we realize that the cost of screws and bolts is more than the original cost of the boat.

Drill, countersink. Not another missed plank!

The scariest job was jacking and pulling planks and ribs together with straps and bolts while simultaneously refastening planks, replacing the mast step and crossbeams, rebuilding ribs, and adding new end blocks. Magically, it all came together (so to speak).

Step 7: Removed long bolts and through-bolted all the planks below the waterline. When done, no cracks between the planks were more than 3/8 of an inch wide.

Drill, countersink, screw, hand-tighten everything near the transom. Go find lights for dark, fall asleep on toilet, forget lights, go to bed. Friends and relatives visited less often, intimidated by threats of work, haggard expressions, and the maniacal visages of the lunatics who once seemed kind of normal. I am unwilling to accept guilt for the wretched state to which I had enslaved myself.

Drill, countersink, screw, hand-tighten, maybe it needs just a few more fasteners.

Step 8: Patch-filled wood and resealed damaged areas before final tightening to solidify the hull.

Drill, countersink, screw, hand-tighten. It doesn't need more, right? We passed out of the ICU (Intensive Care Unit) stage, and the vessel could be classified as "critical but stable." We had reached the bottom, and we began to put her together again.

Drill, countersink, screw, 1,300 screws and bolts in 10 weeks while sanding, cleaning, and rebuilding. George finished his magic and the " show-stoppers," the rotted crossbeams, mast step, ribs, decks, and transom, were history.

Desperately, we rushed to finish plugging holes, patching damage, and sanding and finishing the edges and joints. We wanted to get at least one coat of primer on before colder weather could deprive us of these few meager victories.

Refastening a hull is not a job I would recommend, but it *can* be done if you can keep at it long enough with plenty of help. The most difficult part was forcing the hull back into a usable shape. We saved an old boat, but it must have been during the fall of 1997 that I traded in my

Stripping, patching, sanding, and filling to get a solid and fair surface was easy after what we went through to refasten the hull. Nonetheless, it still needed plenty of work after the paint was put on to look smooth and fair.

normally effective bifocals for the *Rose*-colored glasses my wife wears. With the hull now a unified structure, the saga continued and we began to plan *Rose's* restoration.

> *The hull refastening was done,*
> *and we reassured ourselves that*
> *"Wherever the keel goes,*
> *the rest of the boat will go, too!"*
> *Somehow the pride in that statement*
> *was lost on our audience.*

3

THE CAVALRY ARRIVES

As we began to survey the vessel, we were overwhelmed with tasks that we didn't have a clue how to complete. It was obvious that I was in way over my head. The good news was that lots of family and friends rallied around to see what I had gotten myself into.

Back when we began the refastening and the heat soared over 90 degrees, I became convinced the boat would be better off as a grandchildren's playhouse. It could be painted green and orange, with a Jolly Roger flying from the poop deck, and an opening on the side with climbing handholds and a gangway. I'd use a hammock to laze away summer days in our glade while watching the kids play.

However, Cheryl hovered near the derelict's ravaged body, reaffirming my dedication to the tasks at hand and the futility of such thoughts. Later, when I began obsessing about *Rose* as the centerpiece for our Fourth of July party, Cheryl resolved the crises with a stream of visitors to encourage me in my labors.

Time and again, Cheryl was the driving force and spirit. Her dream became the blueprint for *Rose*. She, more than anyone, is responsible for that derelict becoming *Rose*.

It was critical to fix the "show stoppers," the rotted crossbeams, mast step, ribs, decks, and transom, or we would not have a boat at all. We were overwhelmed and we needed help.

Rob "The Toolman" Duff, my son-in-law, was a notable volunteer. When we gave him a powerful saw for his birthday, he unpacked it, plugged it in, and used it to cut the birthday cake!

I have heard of the generation gap, but it was never more clear than when I handed Rob an old manual screwdriver. He looked at it as if he were eyeing a Neanderthal loose in the twenty-first century. He then gave it back, whipped out an 18-volt drill-driver with infinitely variable, adjustable ratcheting clutch-drive and an automatic tool ejector chuck as he walked to his "Tool-Wagon" for a hardened screwdriver tip with microclamping serrated edges.

Minutes after I had handed him the ordinary screwdriver for an eight-second job, he pressed the 5-pound drilling system into the screw head. Then, looking to make sure I was watching his smug smile, he squeezed the trigger on his weapon of choice to seat the thoroughly overwhelmed screw.

In our most desperate hour, Rob earned the coveted Circle of the *Rose* Award. He and I stood shoulder-to-shoulder and refastened the hull with hundreds of bolts and screws.

My son David, a powerful man who stands 6 feet, 2 inches tall and can wield a grinder over his head, was another serious contributor. His size and strength is matched by innovation, personality, and his experience in the navy. He claimed he had spent so much time chipping and painting "real boats" (457 feet long), that playing with a 25-footer was no challenge. His sense of humor and upbeat manner kept us going through the rough spots. He is loved as our family comedian, and his stand-up routines are legendary.

Of course, my daughter Jennifer was always my best supporter. Daughters have a knack of knowing that everything Daddy does is deserving of disdain, so I was never able to disappoint her, an invaluable attribute when challenged by *Rose*. Jennifer is also one heck of a worker, and she wields a mean 18-volt drill driver. She resisted the temptation to assassinate the Chief Protector after a memorable fiasco one rainy night in Annapolis. Jennifer has built a reputation for saving our butts over the years and her name is written all over the *Rose* story.

My eldest son Stephen contributed his enthusiasm and generous smile as well as many hours of work during *Rose*'s exile in Pennsylvania. He often joined the other two guys and, between ribbing each other continually, these three provided the half-dozen hands needed for the large projects.

My brother Tom looks just like my dad, and he inherited many of Dad's talents. He saved me many times when anything mechanical was the issue, including motors, metal working, and welding, though I had to put up with his incredulous looks as he listened to my wild ideas and theories.

Tom also contributed my father's massive 40-year-old rotary grinder at a critical time. This supposedly handheld machine was from a period when men were men, and machines were scary. Mounted with grinding disks, it is suitable for removing anything and all the guys had to prove their machismo with it for at least a few minutes.

Days of work with the grinder, scrapers, and sanders revealed white cedar planks discolored by the years and damaged by the flailing, grinding disks. Each slip of the disk dug a hole about a 1/4 inch deep into the cedar of the deck and hull, creating more filling and sanding work for later. It also caused equally impressive damage to humans. The disks seemed to enjoy human flesh on days when the temperature exceeded 90 degrees and the bugs were already feasting on the burned flesh, nicely seasoned with sweat and an 1/8 inch of paint, asphalt dust, and debris.

Many helped, but few had real experience with the *Rose*'s problems. I voraciously digested books and magazines, trying to figure out what to do, but we needed some serious expertise. As they say in old western movies, we needed a gunslinger.

Enter the *Dynamic Duo*, Mike Haines and George Hazard, from Haines Restorations, a famous furniture and boat restoration firm just down the road in West Chester.

Rob "The Toolman" Duff, my son-in-law, did one heck of a lot of work on Rose.

Mike is a gregarious guy who wields expertise as a social weapon. His mellow humor and insights helped to guide us, and then he asked George to take care of us. It was clear that I was going to learn a lot working with George, if I could afford it. I recall a plumber's price quote: "$95 per hour, $105 per hour if you watch, and $125 per hour if you help." Incredibly, George didn't charge extra if I helped him. (However, I did slow him down, so I left him alone to finish the repairs.) Though I never saw him in shining armor, and his steed was a blue-on-blue pickup, George was a hero. He knew about wood, woodworking, sailing, and wooden sailing boats. He also knew about fixing them.

He tackled one task after another, and I learned by watching. I noticed the use of an opposing thumb on each hand. He knew how to apply tools to wood in such a manner that the wood would change its shape as desired. This was a real eye-opener. He also gave me the confidence and tips to do many tasks on my own.

The first major challenge was the keel crossbeams, ribs, and mast step amidships. This was crucial for later bolting the hull back together since one of the reasons it had fallen apart was the damage to this part of the structure. George created new, laminated ribs from mahogany to interface with the remains of the oak ribs. He notched the good wood of the ribs so each laminate laid into the notch like a series of steps. Then he through-bolted the entire mess to the hull with plastic to prevent the epoxy from gluing the rib to the planks. When done, he dismantled the assembly, we refilled the holes, and *voilá*, the new ribs were stronger and better than the originals.

Next, George replaced the crossbeams and mast step with massive, white oak components carved with a rotary hand saw and fitted in two trips below. This process would have taken me days. It took him three hours. He then sealed each component in epoxy and through-bolted them to each other, as well as to the keel and the ribs. Now the mast step would go wherever the keel goes, which is considered a good thing in boating circles.

It was harder than it looked since the hull was falling apart as we performed this surgery. At the same time, we steadily performed an engineering miracle by reshaping and refastening the hull in concert with George's rebuilding.

George was my mild mannered Super Carpenter, mentor, and cheering section. As the bad news piled up, George just kept smiling and plugging along. It cost more than *Rose*'s total outlay to date for his expertise, but without it we certainly would have floundered at this stage in the process.

Concentrating down toward the bilges didn't fix all the problems that we needed him to cure. The king planks (two center planks) from the bow to the leading edge of the cabin had rotted in several places. George had to rip out the king planks and replace them from the bow to the cabin edge with new white cedar planks and complex cuts that fit together perfectly. He rebuilt and replaced pieces of underframes and supports with 1-inch marine ply and sealed it with epoxy to prevent rot. Expert carpentry was the solution for such challenges, and the cost of restoration doubled before he was done.

However, all the books in the world would never have gotten me through that period. With George's expertise and example, the books made some sense. I was able to fix problems, and over the next few years, turn a disaster into a fully restored boat.

The process of refastening seemed unending and George worked his magic. As I learned more of the ills that wooden boats are subject to, and the ways to prevent them, I designed replacement components for future installation.

As George finished off the front deck, we enlarged the hatch area for a new forward hatch and my first woodworking project.

As we removed damaged areas, we analyzed *why* it had become damaged in the first place. In most cases, we were able to diagnose and at least minimize the original problem.

For example, the king planks from the bow to the cabin had extensive damage, and we decided this was due to crosscuts for bollards, hatch, mast hole, and cabin edge. Each crosscut was an invitation for leaks and water to be absorbed by the end grain of the soft cedar. In addition, the structure itself was weakened due to the openings, allowing the deck to flex the most at exactly those locations, and assuring a quicker failure of the caulking and seals.

There was no collar around the mast hole, so the mast and wedges worked on wood edges, damaging the wood while assuring water would be pressed into locations that would never dry out.

George cured the foredeck problems and left what seemed to be a minor problem for later. The foredeck butted up against the leading edge of the

George Hazard, master carpenter, as he starts work to save the transom and artistically create a new, massive toe rail.

cabin. There was some damage that seemed to be okay when we redid the foredeck, so we left the cabin edge job for later.

It turned out to be a little more than a minor problem, but by then I was better equipped and trained to do the job. The next year I rebuilt the area around the cabin front, though I cheated and used a bit more caulk and filler than what would have met with George's approval.

The transom and poop deck were George's next major jobs to tackle. The rotted stern toe-rail was barely attached to the boat and huge gaps around the transom testified that the caulk simply amplified dry-rot damage.

We wanted a substantial stern rail to be used as a mounting platform for cleats and hardware. I was drawing a design when George showed up with a big hunk of mahogany. He politely glanced at my plan, listened to what I thought, then dismissed me with a smile and a flurry of activity. He grabbed his rotary handsaw and began hacking at the mahogany while he tore the stern apart. After a few hours of wrecking, measuring, trimming, and chopping, he had fashioned an interlocking assembly of compound, curved wood that looked great around the transom and poop deck. I cleaned and sanded the transom and dug out all the rot and old caulk so he would have somewhere for it to bond and attach. I never did finish the plan.

After a few days of finishing and fitting to the rest of the vessel, the rail, deck, and transom were all much better. I assure you I never would have finished that job, much less had it perfect in three days.

George and Mike also contributed to our emotional well-being. We still keep in touch; a friendly smile and a tidbit of advice from time to time has been a great benefit of the *Rose* affair.

I learned a lot,
and got to know and love many people
because of Rose.
Maybe it was about people all along.

4

A PROJECT PLAN
IN *ROSE*'S DUNGEON

As autumn closed in with exotic colors and frosty winds slipping between the evergreens, our first summer drew to a close. We sealed the hull with primer and covered the topsides with tarps. The boat was not going downhill as fast as before, but in a sense, she had not improved much either. She was not seaworthy, had no interior, and no way to move. She looked no better from afar and our best work was hiding under primer. Parts and rigging were strewn about her interior, and our claim to progress was, "Wherever the keel goes, the rest of the boat will go too."

As the tortuous summer passed, our tools were jammed onto a commandeered picnic table under *Rose*'s bowsprit. We referred to the various piles of stuff as staging area #1 (our back porch), staging area # 2 (our dining room), and staging area #3 (our garage). The mess was not good for work and it was bad for morale, especially mine.

When I was younger, I dreamed of a beautiful workshop with lots of space and tools; it was the envy of all. By 1997, that reality had not come to pass.

Before we got the boat, my few tools hid in the garage and they were barely adequate for automobile, home, or bicycle repairs. My tools were so poor, my friends and relatives brought their own tools when they came to work on *Rose*. Most were shocked by the deplorable state of our home. The backyard had degenerated into a 100x100-foot disaster area, and debris trailed onto our patio and into every room in our house. I felt the lack of a workshop keenly, and I pressed to get tools, parts, and a place to work.

Despite poor accessibility, *Rose*-related implements and supplies were hauled into the basement. It was as if the house reserved this spot as *Rose*'s den. There were few lights, and it was nicknamed *Rose*'s Dungeon. We added lights and power outlets, but the name stuck. It also has water and ventilation problems since it is below ground with no opening windows. To remedy that problem, we drove a 1-foot square hole through a 2-foot concrete wall on the northeast corner to install a fan.

We organized the shop along a north-south axis, about 55 feet long with the furnace to the south. We set up a large 4-foot x 8-inch stainless steel–topped table in the center and a row of workbenches along the east wall. The drill press and miter-cut saw sit close to the workbench. Shelves run parallel along the west wall for hand tools, with the table saw and router to the north. There is also plenty of wood storage that is capable of storing large pieces of wood.

Toward the east side there's a painting area that is ducted to outside. The milling machine/drill press was south of the large workbench, with the grinding/sanding table. The wider area near the furnace gave us room for shelves and space for the electric propulsion system development lab.

The grinding and polishing center has three grinders and a 1-inch stationary belt sander backed up by a portable rotary sander/grinder. This workbench was mounted on wheels so it could be moved and even act as a stand for large pieces.

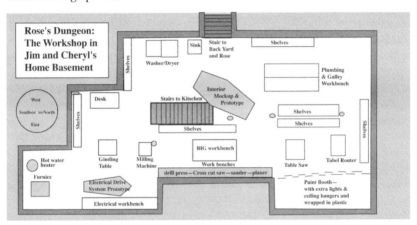

My brother Tom gave me a milling machine, which carves metal, wood, or any material. With a transport table, it does exacting work that other tools such as a router or drill press can't match. The compound miter saw worked right out of the box, and it greatly improved fit and finish.

Foot-activated on/off switches help for quality and safety. I use the foot switch for the table saw. I can turn it off easily, and the starting maneuver of positioning hands and feet forces me to consider (for a split second) what I am doing with my body. Stop and think, slow down, and reconsider are all good dictums. If a switch helps remind me, then it is good.

One problem with power tools is the wood; it seems content to just lie there until it feels threatened, then it suddenly displays its ability to move and tries to get away. I believe that clamps do not hold an unresisting piece of wood in place, but instead they prevent it from escaping in a frantic bid for freedom when a power tool starts to howl. Clamps and jigs are the first step, but it may take longer to manufacture a jig to entrap a piece of wood than it would take to work on the wood. I bought clamps—spring-loaded clamps, wood clamps, short clamps, long clamps, and looooong clamps. I usually plant a 30-pound vise on top to hold things still.

Rose's Dungeon was my second home for many hours of work. This view shows the spar project on benches on the left, tool shelves in the background, main work table in the center, and the table saw in the foreground.

Since I doubled the lights, I drop things less frequently, trip fewer times, lose fasteners and tools less often, and do a better job. The result is fewer accidents, Band-Aids, and less time at the first-aid station. I am a convert—more lights. Everywhere in a shop, there should be enough light to read a book.

Around the southern side, I built storage for parts, supplies, and mockups. As we fumbled our way through this project, tradeoffs of position and size on each new task were intimidating. The mockups permitted us to make decisions like these using cheaper wood, which became the templates for cutting the high-quality wood when the design was final. The interior cabin mockup did encroach on the clothes washing area, but Cheryl simply hung clothes on it, so we got along okay.

We discovered in our first mockup that guys could not do the stand-up thing in the toilet since big feet didn't fit on the small floor to balance and aim; gals could not do the sit-down thing because the seat was too high for short legs. The mockup also showed how plumbing and hoses could fit, which saved us a lot of work, joints, and fitting.

There were other projects with a specific area for tools and parts on the southern side as well. Easy-to-carry crates were used to carry tools and parts back and forth to *Rose*. We now had a workshop and some tools. Our confidence level was better, though our skills were still lagging.

Over the past five years, *Rose*'s Dungeon was a perfect den for making *Rose* what she is today. Yet, it never vaguely resembled the beautiful shop I dreamed of when I was younger. I do know that 1,500 square feet was barely enough space.

We rediscovered our dining room table and began to outfit the shop. Cheryl is good at acquiring nearly everything we need. She has tried to

Rose

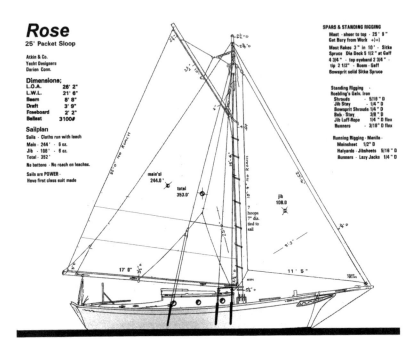

We made an important decision to retain the gaff rig with one foresail (roller-furling jib) as designed, along with rigging and exterior appearance, as above.

educate me in the art of shopping, especially since my skills in that activity were almost nonexistent when we started working on *Rose*. I often get lost or bellow for help, which may create a bit of a scene. Cheryl even ditched me once when I tried to negotiate a price at a department store.

I collected catalogues, hoping they might save me. Without even leaving the house, I could place large orders that would show up at my home later. I tried selecting one of everything, but the budget disappeared within a few pages.

My shopping failure led to a new strategy, buy only when needed. According to scholars, man is a tool-making animal—I think man is a tool-*buying* animal. However, if I was going to be sensible about shopping, I really needed a plan.

We had piles of books, catalogues, magazines, and photographs to get started on our planning. We collected all kinds of *stuff* and visited every booth at the Annapolis Boat Show, the Wooden Boat Festival, and boat flea markets that summer and fall.

We imagined and discussed what *Rose* was supposed to be as we dismantled her, and ideas began to crystallize. A portfolio of drawings grew and became a box full of drawings and "good" junk. We began collecting pictures and notes as well. We were determined that others should know what we were going through; our determination was what started this book.

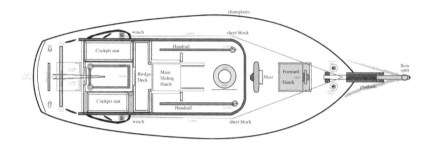

Open, broad decks were in bad shape but had lots of potential. We restored them as we wanted and kept the layout as simple as possible.

We decided to restore *Rose* to the original design and retain the gaff rig, though we were inclined toward a more traditional look than when she was launched in 1960. We were also facing the prospect of rebuilding, restoring, and customizing to fit our needs. We needed electrical, plumbing, and propulsion systems. There were dozens of projects to be done and we thought we would be done in about two years.

I started a project plan and design drawings. Some of these were transferred to the computer. We also scanned blueprints and pictures from articles to update them in the computer as well.

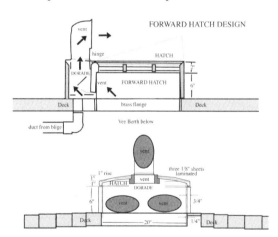

We drew over 50 different component plans, such as the forward hatch design above. This detail was necessary to find and cut materials properly and to complete construction that actually worked and looked good. A forward mahogany hatch works well and keeps us dry with a traditional appearance, emergency access, safety, strength, and ventilation. Attaching it securely to the forward deck was a major challenge (see Chapter 15).

I needed a plan. It's just a thing with me, the engineer. I had to have it—despite the fact that I accept that a plan is a carefully designed process of what might happen only if the world works the way we want it to.

Obviously, some features were dropped in the restoration, such as a binnacle compass, ugly ventilators on each side of the cockpit, and the gas engine. We replaced stainless cable shrouds on the bowsprit with chains that look great and are easier to brace feet and hands on. The boom gallows behind the cockpit was moved aft so the pilot can sit on the poop deck for a better view. The forward hatch departs from the designer's intentions, but we hope he would have been pleased with our contribution to *Rose*'s history.

Even before *Rose* landed in the yard, we wanted an electric propulsion system. An electric motor would replace the gas engine with battery banks under the berth. When we started, it sounded too good to be true, and it was.

The original interior layout bothered us at the start. There was a huge berth forward, with a sizable head in the center on the port side. One might have thought the original owners were large people, if not for a small seat and a tiny table that folded down. Two people could not sit, much less dine, inside. We theorized that the original owner might have sailed long distances singlehanded. Oversized fuel and water tanks reinforced the idea.

When the interior had to be pulled out, we that felt a new interior might better fit the boat so we felt no guilt about not preserving the original. We wanted a layout with a traditional appearance as well as all the space and comfort we could fit.

Basically, we wanted to redo it as a "pocket cruiser." We looked forward to short cruises near shore-based facilities and comfortable day sailing with one of our children's families or another couple. We wanted flexible space with movable curtains, a table, and a ladder.

Our first demand was a salon, then a stateroom, dinette, galley, and head. The plan was to tuck a small toilet space on the port side, with a minigalley starboard. Settees on either side, around a folding table, frame the forward V-berth and act as couches too. The design makes the spaces flexible and interchangeable.

We didn't want modern conveniences to clash with the traditional. This desire led to some strange bedfellows—carved shelves to house the hand-held GPS and VHF radio, near a bronze stove and an antique brass chest labeled "First Aid."

Cabinetry was built in modular fashion, so the pieces would fit through the main hatch for assembly in the cabin. We dabbled with changes and redesigns on mockups, inching toward something that would work. The designs evolved as we realized that a cool idea was a lot of work or that a part was expensive. Some changes were opportunistic, such as finding cool thingamajigs in a flea market that simply *had* to be on the boat.

I organized drawings, pictures, and notes into a scrapbook to share our dream and buoy our spirits. I drew a colored picture of what *Rose* was supposed to look like. So much effort and money was invested by then that

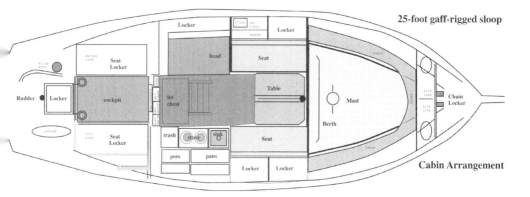

Cabin Arrangement

A new interior layout was needed before we could really plan the restoration. We experimented with a half-dozen major design variations and hundreds of minor items to finally get it all together. The mockup was indispensable.

I had to finish the restoration. As 1997 drew to a close, *Rose* was on her way back up, though it would be a long time before she went back to the sea. Amidst the bold colors of autumn, the diagnosis of Woody Disease became unarguably positive; maybe it was a good year after all.

My friends smilingly ignored me when I pointed out that there was still a lot of work to be done. They were safe behind the knowledge that even a rube like me could not expect them to work in the cold of winter out in the backyard.

So, protected by the mantle of Old Man Winter's upcoming aura, they could be our friends for a few months before the lunacy would surface again. Who knows? We might even return to normal by then.

I am reminded that a good plan is a starting point, not the end.
A friend of mine offers two appropriate sayings:
"Life is what happens when we're planning something else" and
"If you want to give God a chuckle, tell Him your plans."

I also realized that money spent on tools and parts
will not produce good work. I had to become a craftsman.

5

INSIDE A *ROSE*

Rose was ready for her first winter only after primer protected her hull planks, which were freshly fastened to her ribs, which were attached to her keel just like a real boat. Varnish embraced her repaired transom and trim, and a coat of sealer covered the decks.

Painting the inside of the hull was a task of highest priority. We didn't want to put our new interior on top of a nasty-looking hull. It is also wise to seal the wood on all sides, to ensure the moisture content is even.

We faced hundreds of square feet of interior wood to be filled and painted, but nuts and bolts protruded from the ribs. The trusty grinder and several days of work yielded a usable surface that would never pass as a work of art.

However, we couldn't figure out how to paint the undersides of decks and the many tiny places without spraying. The acquisition of a paint sprayer and breathing equipment moved us into a new arena of offensive technology.

Trapped inside the closed space, the spray paint quickly plugged my breathing filters. Unable to draw air through the filters, I began to suck air around the edges of the mask and my breath fogged the inside of the glasses so I could not see.

An hour of awkward work spraying paint inside the rounded hull in 80-degree heat produced a nice try at heat stroke and asphyxiation. Pain and suffering followed as I tried to remove impregnated spray paint from ears, nostrils, flesh, and hair.

I never tried to spray again. It is better to endure hand-painting than to face that ordeal. It does prove that bad equipment is worse than none. This job should be done with full-face masks and tanks, not with the usual equipment found at the local Home Depot. Though I was in no condition to appreciate it, my dangerous work yielded a moderately attractive interior. It was ready for through-hull fittings and ceilings.

We designed the layout for our intended use, while making it seem as if it were originally designed for the boat. One goal was to improve space utilization without hurting the look and feel of the boat. The plan was to tuck a small toilet space as far aft as possible on the port side to free up space for everything else. A minigalley faces that, on the starboard side across the companionway ladder and the open space in the middle of the cabin.

This open space is used as the open space for any part of the cabin. For example, with the ladder moved out of the way, the open area can be used as a nice, large galley. With the ladder in place and the table moved out, the open space makes a large bedroom reaching forward to the berth. We can even divide off the back section with a curtain and use the toilet area, the open space, and the sink in the galley as a bathroom with the shower in the hatch over the open area.

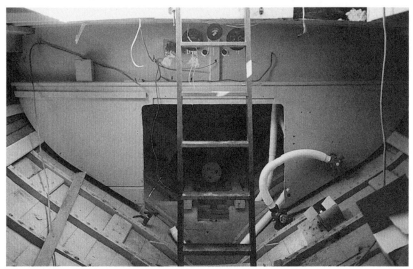

The interior was removed when the hull was rebuilt, except for the main bulkhead at the bridge deck and cockpit. (The main hatch to the cockpit is at the top of the picture and the engine compartment is behind the ladder.) Once the hull was sealed and painted, the installation of ceilings, a floor, a new interior, and electrical, plumbing, and mechanical systems could begin.

A settee fits on either side amidships, with a folding table and a V-berth forward. We designed the largest dinette we could squeeze in with a solid and attractive table that is removable and folds down easily. The settees could be used as couches with the table out of the way.

Building a mockup was one thing, but the components had to be built in a modular fashion so the pieces would fit through the hatch to be assembled in the cabin during installation.

The interior bulkheads are 1/2-inch marine plywood with a Lloyd's registry certificate on the surface. We had no problem with this wood, though we did have trouble with other "marine plywood" that delaminated.

The final appearance had to seem integrated and finished, so lots of energy went into designs and mockups. They sat in the basement for months as we dabbled with changes and redesigns.

I thought the ceilings would be a straightforward job, but I could not find the cedar desired by the designer. The closest thing we could come up with were precut pieces for closets, which were too short to look good over a large area and too wide to be attractive anywhere.

We extended the ceilings to enclose the inner side of the hull for a warm, finished look while it also strengthened the hull. I chose strips of mahogany where the ceilings were visible and used cedar under cabinets, berths, and seats. We cut the mahogany into 50 5/16-inch-thick pieces that were 2 inches wide and up to 12 feet long. It was noisy, dusty, and dangerous because the fragile strips whipped about in the confined spaces of the basement. We sanded the pieces before varnishing. After installation, we sealed the ends and revarnished everything.

This is the kind of work I will pay a milling shop to do in the future. I admit that the major task I accomplished was to convert expensive wood into expensive sawdust. This led to another problem in the confines of *Rose's* Dungeon. The shop layout let dust from the power tools settle into the furnace, prompting foul language from the heater man.

Looking toward the focs'l after the mahogany ceilings were installed above the waterline. Cedar ceilings below the waterline are partially installed in the bow and will be hidden beneath the berth and settees. A 2-inch space between the ceilings and the hull permits airflow from the bilge between the ribs to control the moisture content of the hull planks at a steady level.

It also prompted me to collect the sawdust into piles in the corner farthest from the heater, with the intention to haul it away someday. However, I warily eyed the mushrooming mass as it grew more threatening over the weeks. Some days I didn't work in the dungeon, but the pile still seemed to grow larger. Note that I live in Downingtown; its claim to fame is that the diner in town was used as the prop for the 1950s sci-fi flick *The Blob*. As winter dragged on, the pile continued to grow as if it took on a life

Bulkheads, three battery boxes, and a dozen batteries temporarily installed under the berth as final fitting and attachment details are worked out. The challenge was to attach everything to keep 780 pounds of batteries from flying around the interior in heavy going, while providing access to every component, wire, and hose for mainte- nance and emergencies.

of its own, like the Blob. At the current rate of growth, it was clear that it would ingest important works of art, or perhaps the whole interior mockup, long before it was completed and then take over the basement well before the boat was done.

As snow closed down the outside basement door, I took the precaution of withdrawing tools and storage shelves from the leading edges of the pile. This cautious retreat was a prelude to a full-scale rout as the pile surged forward, adding territory in a fashion familiar to aficionados of the Blitzkrieg.

I hoped that in spring I could retreat to the backyard, but by February the situation was critical. A sweetly rank odor emanated from the bulging mass, reminiscent of a still of white lightning. Further appeasement was intoler- able, so with help, the pile was strewn across the backyard, and we saved the shop.

As spring arrived, I dragged my wonderful components out to *Rose* and began the installation. I quickly discovered two problems: the human body and gravity in a rounded, hull form. Materials and the human body try to comply with gravity, but with no flat place to stand, sit, or lie in an unin- stalled interior, everything fumbles to the bottom.

The best I could do was precariously balance a few seconds in some untenable position, drill a hole, and drop a nail in place to hold stuff, then move to another perch for a few seconds. What I expected to be an easy job on a flat surface took four days.

Two partial-side bulkheads are key structures that act as mounting plates for other interior components, including settees in front of them with lockers over, and the toilet area and galley in back of them. They also have to look nice, and feel strong and comfortable, so heavy teak trim was added later.

When we installed ceilings, I left a 2-inch section open at the top edge, so air could flow up between the ribs and the inside of the hull to exhaust into the cabin.

I replaced the damaged chainplates with suitable constructs at the same time. Since the hull was damaged by the rotting bolts on the chainplates, we added new oak stringers along the interior that the new chainplates bolted through with five bolts instead of three.

We had to raise the berth to make everything fit, which was not a problem, and made it easier to install the salon table and climb in and out of the forward hatch.

Three bulkheads pass through the area, a small removable one forward, a second large removable one 18 inches forward of the mast, and a large permanent one 18 inches aft of the mast. These bulkheads act as supports for the berth and as attachment points for lines and equipment under the berth.

I also discovered a wood boat construction principle. No piece of wood fits in the interior of a vessel in one attempt. I cut wood in the basement, then finished and sealed it with urethane, only to destroy it in 20 minutes of trimming onboard. The two partial bulkheads that formed the edges between the settees, the galley, and the toilet area were particularly trying.

The head was a gruesome fitting job since the space was very small. It was competing with the galley, the settee, and the companionway for accessibility. We wanted access to the heavy weather gear locker, plumbing, electrical, and drive systems, yet we also wanted spots for goodies close to the hatch.

After the partial bulkheads were fitted, I cut a set of frames for the toilet area flooring, carefully fitted each piece, and finished them with urethane. While it was drying, I installed the plumbing, which took longer than expected. Then we were shut down with five days of rain. When I returned to install the fitted and finished components of the toilet area, nothing fit. After much weeping and gnashing of teeth, followed by cursing and bellowing, I realized that five days of rain caused the boat to change shape more dramatically than I ever would have imagined.

Wood swells in all directions except along the grain, until it runs into constraints that prevent it from swelling along that axis, which causes

The toilet area is extremely small and 6 inches higher than the main cabin sole, with lots of angles and corners. It took three mockups and many fitting templates, since it has 14 pieces of wood that are angled to fit perfectly.

twisting or movement away from the stress point. A combination of these factors may be impossible to predict, though they are understandable after the fact when you examine the disruption the movements caused.

Out of this mess, a lesson can be drawn. It was clear that the interior must be flexible, literally flexible. Essentially, room must be left in the fitting process so that the boat can change shape without breaking joints or fasteners. For example, bulkheads were bolted to the flexible ceiling, so that twisting, turning, shrinkage, or swelling did little damage, while the hull benefited from the strength of the bulkhead. Such observations came a little late, but I refrained from tightening everything firmly until the boat was in the water and had adjusted.

With bulkheads in place, we placed battery boxes and removable bulkheads and then finished the berth area. After a few days of work, the settees were done and the layout of the interior was visible.

When we started to save *Rose*, I worked hard sealing the wood hull to keep water out. When I was done and had no leaks, I punched holes in the hull so we could let water in. Then, for a twist, we punched holes so we could pump water out again. (For a complete account of Rose's plumbing, see Chapter 12.)

It took many more parts and a lot more work than I could have imagined to create a legitimate interior that was strong, flexible, useful, and attractive, but it was worth it.

> *I admit that the plumbing on* Rose *strained my*
> *patience and vocabulary on more than one occasion.*
> *Worst of all, nobody is going to come aboard,*
> *stick their head into the locker spaces, and pronounce,*
> *"Gee, Jim, I really like the way you did the plumbing!"*

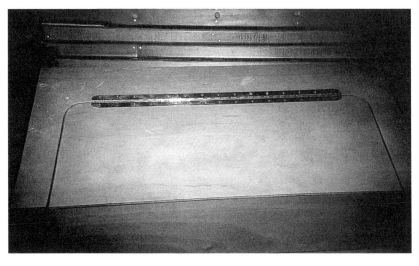

Two settees with stowage behind and lockers beneath face each other amidships. They fit between the low bulkhead at the berth (upper right), the toilet, and galley areas.

6

ROSE'S SPARS:
YOU WANT ME TO
PUT THESE WHERE?

Refurbishing the spars seemed a straightforward task, so it became my first large job in the basement. Amazingly, the bowsprit, two booms, and mast fit through the basement door and into the cavernous space that had been hiding beneath our house for the last 50 years.

I organized the shop so we had a 20-foot counter on 2x5-inch workbenches on the east wall, which became the spar refurbishment project area.

The lines, standing and running rigging, rings, pulleys, and hardware had to be removed and stored for refurbishment and reinstallation. As we disassembled, we were mystified by all the worn and battered pieces. I cautiously labeled components to make sure I'd get it back together later. This detailed labeling required drawings to make sense of the labels. It was fortunate that I took these precautions, since it took five years to rebuild the boat, and I had forgotten it all by the time we rigged it.

One of the worst parts of this job was trying to remove corroded parts without further damaging the wood. It was not just the rusted screw holes; in many cases the hole was only a fraction of the size of the damage. It seemed that every screw or item touching the wood had left its mark, and it was not pretty.

A number of suspension jigs made from wood and bungee cord held spars and components while we sanded and painted. Even the rafters, as well as any bench and shelf, became fair game during jig building.

Ventilation proved to be a problem, especially while using a heat gun and chemicals. This problem was further exacerbated by the cloud of sawdust and paint dust. I had done little work on the spars before it was clear that the buildup of sawdust, mold, paint, and solvent odors was intolerable. The vapors quickly worked into the house, so we installed a fan to evacuate the air from the paint area to the outside. It was a lifesaver over the next five years.

My small heat gun proved its inability to intimidate the tough paint on the exterior as we rebuilt the hull, so I purchased a new heat gun. Surprisingly, the heat gun and scraper worked. Paint peeled off in long strips to reveal curved wood. A coat of stripper, some scraping, and sanding yielded a surface that needed no apologies when it was coated with a sparkling coat of varnish.

Proud of the achievement, I imagined just how great the spars would look in a few days. Enthusiasm reached new highs as I began the main boom, but the brand-new heat gun died. No warning, just two hours of use, and it died!

Gathering the box, receipts, and manuals, I returned to the retailer only to find they were sold out of that model. They tried to sell me alternatives, so I gave up and went to another store, where I got the same story.

Frustrated by spending more time shopping than working, I got the biggest, most powerful gun for twice the price of the first gun. With power to spare, it quickly charbroiled the paint in small areas, producing smoky fumes and flying sparks of burnt wood and paint, while leaving the rest of the paint to glare resistantly at the scraper.

After a lot of experimentation, I found a setting that worked most of the time. I also redesigned and beat a new flare tip that seemed satisfactory. With great care and effort, I could move at about half the speed of the previous smaller, less powerful gun, with twice the expenditure of effort. Worse yet, the process caused the wood to split on fine grains and strip away from the boom. The 6 hours of work needed to prepare the gaff boom became 20 hours to produce an inferior job on the main boom.

Steel rings were solidly rusted onto the top of the mast. There was also a huge teak turning block and many miscellaneous things all over it. The bowsprit was as bad and the two booms had multipart yokes and too many things attached to keep track. It took days to get the parts off and cleaned up.

It also polluted my breathing passages and produced burned fingers, aching shoulders and wrists, and a sore back. The mast was more formidable, and four weeks slipped by before the spars were ready for varnish—four times longer than planned.

The bowsprit is a critical spar, but its treatment was more interesting than the mast and booms. Cheryl had determined that no matter what its function, it should look like mahogany to match the rails. It should not look like the orange varnish of the standing spars once we got the many pounds of old stuff off it.

The right tool is critical—too much power is just as bad as too little power. However, skill is even more important. A plethora of factors are involved in the art of stripping: the direction of the air stream relative to the surface and the blade, the speed of scraping, the amount of preheating, the type and thickness and condition of the paint, the condition of the wood beneath the paint, the direction of the grain, the damage to the surface, and even the room's temperature and air flow.

I discovered that the grain of wood is quite variable. The grain can rise to the surface, causing the scraper to dig in, and then turn the other way in just a few inches. There was no blend of airflow, temperature, or blade angle that worked under all circumstances.

The bowsprit was finished differently than other spars. This was the first setup, after we changed it. Note two bollards at the back, the side, and bottom chains and small custom-built anchor capstan.

The only technique that seemed generally useful was to warm up an area 8 to 10 inches long, and maybe 6 inches high. Carefully start at one end of that area, with the heat gun held close to the scraper blade, and move steadily. I used my body to slow things down, rather than my arm, which tended to go too fast. Then I moved the blade up or down slightly and repeated the stroke. The excess heat from the last stroke tended to warm the strip next to it. By the third stroke, the motion was steady and the removal process became fairly effective.

My words of wisdom are to take your time, experiment a lot, and be careful. No matter how successful the heat gun technique, a thin layer of paint still adhered to the wood, often in the grain or imperfections, so some alternate was needed to finish it off. Chemical stripper worked fairly well, but the scraping process only offered more opportunities to dig into the grain and still left spots with paint imbedded in the wood. A light sanding with sandpaper or steel wool prepared the wood for a good wash with spirits, leaving a decent surface.

Sanding was the final step, with extra care on spots with paint, since they are harder and sand more slowly than wood, causing an uneven surface. A long straightedge helped find high and low spots for doctoring.

Despite the attention, any number of nasty wounds in the surface insulted my eyes. Sometimes it was a dark watermark or a deep gouge, but many spots had both problems. If they were small and shallow enough, sanding was a cure, though this meant sanding an area 3 feet long to remove the unevenness created by a 3-inch-long wound.

If the wood looked generally good, but there was a water stain with no gouging, I found that household bleach took out stains without damaging the wood. Some spots were so badly gouged that my options were clear: ignore it or fix it. I humbly admit to applying some epoxy filler to those spots with a sprinkling of sawdust from surrounding wood, so that the varnish would not highlight the repair. I also selected a stain to help blend the edges of the repairs.

A traditional wood rig with wood yokes, leather, and wood hoops radiates a kind of majesty in appearance, strength, and sound. Surprisingly, it seems to work better than metal components, though it is more maintenance.

Some spots were so bad that a fill job was not right, so I carved a notch into the spar up to several inches long and spliced a piece of wood in as a fix. This technique worked because there was a piece of scrap Sitka spruce in the boat from a broken preventer pole; otherwise, this would have been a nasty-looking repair.

Of course, tools and wood and fasteners will not yield good results until the repaired spars look worthy of the vessel.

The yoke ends were damaged and split, with some holes drilled in them. I cleaned up the mess, and filled and repaired the damage with epoxy reinforced with sawdust. It looked and felt strong, but I would discover that it's hard to fix wood without also fixing the problem.

The bowsprit was painstakingly stained a dark mahogany, but when the varnish was put on it was too dark. I sanded the stain off and re-stained it a lighter shade before varnishing it. We deviated from the design on the bowsprit by replacing stainless shrouds with 3/8-inch black chain. Admittedly, this is retro at its worst, but it looks cool.

We painted the standing spars with three coats of a formidable finish called Armada, which gives it an orange glow. The tips were then painted with three coats of white enamel over white primer. They came out looking good, and have they weathered well.

The new gaff boom yoke is larger and stronger than the original, with more curve and a longer parrel cord so it will not bind if it gets loose in a blow. The new white oak, hardware, and leather is topped off with white paint for visibility.

The bronze hardware was cleaned and repaired, and most of the galvanized steel or stainless hardware was replaced except for the heavy steel rings and caps. I cleaned, reground, and reshaped them. I even rewelded some points so they were better than the originals. These were primed with four coats of black Rustoleum baked on. They looked great and seem pretty hardy.

The standing rigging was in good shape. We replaced steel chainplates with bronze attached to stainless shrouds. It was very difficult to find the right parts, so the searching and shopping process continues to this day.

We knew we needed new sails and lines, but since we had not sailed the boat, we didn't know what we should have. We held off as long as possible until we had more data and delayed buying new sails until after the shakedown cruise.

It took a bit of shopping, but we did find the wood hoops for the mast from a group that makes them in the United States. (Remember to put them on *before* raising the mast.) The mainsail is lashed to the hoops with lashing twine and left in place for the season. They work well and look wonderful.

We got new lines for the rigging, but once it was rigged we didn't like the modern look and feel of them. We are replacing them, so the lines will be traditional as well.

On our shakedown cruise, the gaff boom yoke cracked in a jamming incident. At first I thought it was inexperience, but the main halyard jammed when lowered, the peak halyard twisted when raised, and the halyards did not work in unison. After fixing, fussing, and analysis, I realized the halyards were badly rigged to start.

This was quite bothersome, since we were concerned about this issue in the beginning. Let's face it, all the lines, booms, pulleys, and halyards are intimidating. Lacking confidence, we hired riggers who apparently ignored the designer's drawings and made quite a mess of the rigging. So much for "expertise."

As a result, I had to redo the setup and rerigged the halyards myself. Then I had to rebuild the gaff boom yoke, associated hardware, and accessories. This was a big price to pay for letting the experts do the job.

Fixing the broken gaff boom required dismantling and manufacturing two new matching yoke halves. I made these slightly heavier and stronger than the originals. The new yokes are slightly longer, with a larger end around the hole for the parrel line, which threads through 1-inch-diameter wood beads called "parrels" and strengthens the area.

As an interesting aside, have you ever wondered why the ends of spars are painted white while the rest is often varnished or black? The answer occurred to me while learning to sail her, and it was one of those many moments of enlightenment I had working with *Rose*. I realized that the boom ends painted white are easier to see and handle than varnished ones, so when I replaced the broken yoke on the gaff boom, I painted the two yokes white.

Many parts on the original rigging were questionable when it came time to put them back on; some were so worn or beat up I had no confidence in them, some I didn't understand, and some were just plain wrong. I began collecting parts years before, so by the time we started fine-tuning after the shakedown cruise, I had some parts to draw on from my collection in a giant box.

I strongly recommend these procedures to anyone who tries the restoration thing because finding parts is one of the biggest issues we ran into. It takes a lot of brass and bronze to outfit and rig a boat, particularly one with a gaff rig and a classic appearance.

After years of work and detailing, we can proclaim success. It works better than we expected and it looks great!

No clinking or clanging or ringing sounds
reach the ears from our traditional rig.
We share the sounds of nature and the soothing
way the winds and waves interact with the wood of the boat.
Birds also like it, so we get the pleasure of their visits and
the gifts they leave behind on our hatches, decks, and sails.

7

TOPSIDES REBORN

During her nearly 40-year life, *Rose*'s topsides had degenerated from New England winters and Chesapeake Bay summers, as well as from a fair share of abuse, badly executed changes, and poor maintenance. The decks were a multicolored, multitextured, blend of brown, purple, black, and gray, finished and bare wood, interlaced with cracks, filler, caulking, and missing screw plugs.

The deck is a single layer of parallel, longitudinal, white cedar planks nailed to white oak ribs that span from port to starboard rails. The joints between planks were once filled with black caulking, but most of it had long ago given up any pretense of sealing water out, and gaping cracks stood beside joints filled with dirt and multihued fillers.

The toe-rails were beaten and battered, traces of white paint showed but half the varnish was missing, and the rest was almost impregnable from layers of epoxy. Random holes were plugged with debris and painted over.

The bumper rails were broken and splintered, with gashes and pieces of docks and God-only-knows-what imbedded from battles lost with other objects. The stern toe-rail was rotted out, and rot was moving into the deck and transom.

We found a mess when we pulled the fascia board across the front of the cabin. This board was a primary-strength member between the oak cross-beam, the deck planks (ends visible) lying on the crossbeam, and the forward bulkhead of the cabin above the deck planks. The rotted king planks let rot penetrate and compromised the strength of other critical components. Cheryl pointed out that the forward cabin bulkhead was still okay, despite the problems surrounding it. I weakly nodded in agreement.

The mast goes through the deck 8 inches in front of the cabin and chain-plates attach to the hull on both sides of the cabin, near these crossbeams. The bulkhead is a major stiffener component but the attachment between it and the crossbeam is crucial if the stress of the mast and chainplates is to be handled properly in this area.

Leaking deck planks let water to the end grain of the planks. This helped rot the planks, so the disease spread up into the bulkhead, down into the crossbeam, aft into the fascia board, and sideways into the posts. We replaced the bad wood and sealed it so that it would not trap water in the future.

The teak trim was broken, and badly fitted repairs made it look worse. Dozens of objects penetrated or were attached to the deck, toe-rails, cabin, and cockpit coamings. The cockpit coaming and cabin sides were separated from the deck, plugged with old caulk and dirt, then encased in epoxy. The cabin paint was relatively new, but it covered coats of old, cracked paint and canvas that dated to the creation of the boat.

In our first blush of enthusiasm, we tried to induce the layers of varnish and epoxy to release from the surfaces. Despite advertising claims, we had no luck with any stripper, sander, scraper, or heat gun. We resorted to cursing, psychokinetic energy, black magic, and prayer, all to no avail.

Nothing short of our large grinding machine, mounted with a masonry cutting disk, was up to the task. As wood was uncovered, we were aghast at the mess. Ventilator holes were gored out of the deck beside the cockpit. Screw plugs were dislodged, and the deck was perforated with holes and mechanical things. In some spots, damaged wood was rotten.

We replaced two deck planks, repaired a dozen major holes, plugged dozens of others, and filled and sanded up to a 1/4 inch of wood off the deck to get a decent surface. The damage extended under the cabin edges, so we ripped out and replaced half the cabin/deck joints as well.

Expert carpentry was the only viable solution for some challenges, and months passed as the intimidating tasks were completed, leaving other time-consuming and less rewarding tasks for later.

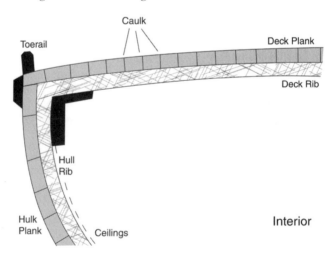

Here, a cross section of single-planked hull and deck structure. The construction technique is the same above and below, but the ability of the deck to keep water out of the interior was very different than the hull. The hull is forced to seal by the wet wood expanding to compress all spaces closed, whereas the deck dries out and shrinks, causing spaces between planks and leaks.

It seemed that the right thing to do was to rip the deck (and cabin) off, redeck with plywood, then put cedar planks back on top of the plywood. (After that, put the cabin back on.) However, we were concerned when we started that the hull might settle and distort further in the process since the deck seemed to be holding the boat together. It also was more work than we were comfortable tackling.

Damage to the king planks and the deck around the bollards demanded new king planks (wide planks in center). The movement of the deck, bollards, and mast damaged the end grain of the white cedar planks, leading to rot.

Once dry rot started, it spread much farther than the original damage, as seen in this underside view of the deck. Though the hull and deck were white cedar, there were no rotten hull planks but several rotten deck planks.

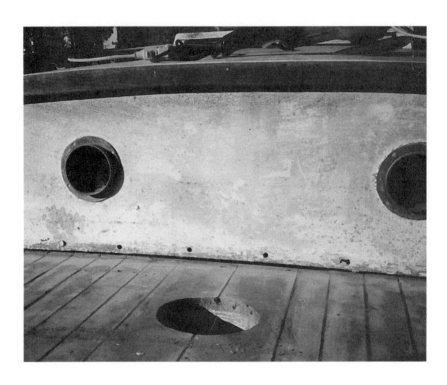

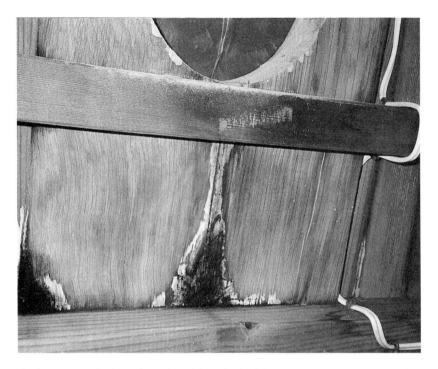

(**Left two images**) *The leading edge of the cabin had damage and major leaks. Outside (above) shows separation between the cabin and deck in the center. Below left shows rot in king planks behind the mast hole, and above shows damage behind the fascia board. King planks and fascia board were replaced and the corners were rebuilt, with new trim inside and out, leaving minor leaks in nasty weather.*

We checked alternatives, such as canvas over the planks, and even bought the canvas, but this seemed wrong since it was neither original nor attractive, and it was more work.

The suggestion of a heavy coating of fiberglass was met with unyielding demands by *Rose*'s guardian that it "look right." Cheryl was committed to the idea of traditional planked decks on *Rose*.

We tried the caulking approach, the selling point being that since the same planked/caulked structure works *under* water, why wouldn't it work *above* water?

We needed to rebuild large sections of the deck before we could refinish it, but we wanted them to last at least 10 years, so we fixed everything properly as we went along. The refinishing effort escalated into a project in just a few days.

Thus began an arduous and frustrating project that spanned years— creating a good-looking and usable wood plank deck with the original wood that was no longer good-looking *or* usable.

As poorly equipped amateurs with no idea how to do it, we did a job several times, with time-wasting indecision between failure and restart. It took 30 months from when we started the topsides for us to complete them. Often the magnitude of each job was so intimidating, we would let it drag on as long as possible. The problems were compounded by a backyard location, dependent on weather and long-term out-of-water storage. In hindsight, we can see that the greatest enemy was us and our high expectations.

Dirt, caulking, and fillers had to be extracted from between deck planks. While it only took about 80 hours of backbreaking labor, we managed to drag it out for at least six months.

For many hours, we picked and cut with all the hand tools and gadgets imaginable, including several homemade tools. The damage we did to the wood and ourselves was not being rewarded with cleaned joints to accept new caulk. We spent hours fixing problems we caused trying to save a few minutes of work. For example, the literature said to tape the deck at the joint, then put the caulk in, pull the tape off, and then sand rubber after it hardened.

A friend assured us that was unnecessary since the decks needed sanding. He showed us how to simply put the caulk in the joints, then sand it off, saving the arduous taping phase. However, the rubber pulled loose from the wood under the torque of the sanding disk, so we had to redo those areas.

We found that tape was not just for appearance, but it reduced the rubber-to-wood bonding surface enough for the sander to do its job. It only cost us about 30 hours of dirty, backbreaking work to discover that little fact the hard way.

One of the challenges was the varying size of the joints between the planks, which made the filling process erratic. Not only did the filler disappear, as if down a bottomless pit at times, but at other places it refused to go anywhere, quickly bubbling up over the deck into a gooey mass.

Even worse, a few hours after being carefully manicured into a smooth, flat surface, the caulk settled unevenly and left deep depressions. This shrinkage factor meant several treatments were necessary. Eventually, we declared the job done and gave up before it ever took on the level of perfection we expected.

As we replaced the king planks, we crafted joints to assure a better seal. We used thicker plywood under the planks, sealed cut ends with epoxy sealer, and reinforced the underdeck area to minimize flexing.

The new hatch design is overengineered to assure a better seal to the deck and reinforce the opening to minimize leaks and flexing. A strong mast collar is bolted around the mast hole, assuring no opportunity for flexing around the hole itself.

The replacement beam across the leading edge of the cabin is wider than the original, and it is mahogany. It extends 3 inches on either side of the original beam, and is through-bolted to the cabin and crossbeam.

Every entrapped surface was sealed with epoxy and 5200 caulking was forced into joints and clamped firmly before bolting. Not only did we minimize the opportunity for water to get trapped in bad places, but we prevented it from doing its dirty deeds once it got there. Such leaks would drip onto the berth, which my spouse clearly informed me was unacceptable.

Similar work was done on the bridge deck between the cockpit and the cabin, and around the lazarette hatch and rudder post. Some areas survived 40 years without damage, so we assured ourselves that the newly repaired areas had an extended lifetime, probably well beyond our own.

We built a larger, more water-resistant lazarette hatch to match the cockpit and rear deck. We used 1/2-inch white cedar so the hatch, seats, and cockpit sole matched the deck nicely, giving the aft section an integrated and traditional appearance.

The original forward hatch was plywood with a hole for a ventilator. The new hatch is high enough to stay above the probable water and a heavy wave over the bow will jam it closed. This gives us some confidence that it will keep the berth drier.

The toe-rails were 1-inch-thick, 3-inch-high mahogany, scarfed together amidships, but the joint on one side was only 11 feet from the bow, and on the other side was almost 13 feet. This nonsymmetry extended to screw placement as well. They trapped up to 2 inches of water, so someone drilled 1-inch-diameter holes at random locations that were plugged with debris.

We felt that two 1x10-inch slits at the deck level were large enough, and we left room for a third slit behind. We discovered toe-rail and deck damage as we worked, which required repair beyond plugging the old holes. The old bolts were galvanized, which corroded and damaged the toe-rails and deck. That damage required hours of work to remove.

A simple drain-hole job became an exercise in reconstruction that lasted two weekends. In hindsight, we could have ripped the old rails off and put new ones on in less time and at a lower cost.

Bumper rails protruding from the sides below the toe-rail had to bridge the joint between deck and hull. They also had to bend around the sheer, which was a real challenge on the complex curved transom. They also had to fit nicely around the chainplates and boarding ladder.

New bumper rails required cutting, bending, trimming, semifinishing, sealing, installation and final finishing. The bending was an opportunity to learn how to bend wood with steam. Incredibly, we could find nothing about the subject and began with little knowledge of what we were doing.

After we finished, we discovered critical knowledge: Kiln-dried wood does not bend well. Steam bending works with green wood, or slightly air-dried wood, but not kiln-dried wood. Apparently, the wood remembers its shape, loses resiliency, and has weaker cross-grain bonds, so it splits easier.

Our first attempt to bend the compound-curved transom bumper rail was a big, steam-bending failure. It began splitting just as it completed the difficult bend around the transom with a dozen clamps helping its journey.

After months of work, and three deck resealings, the topsides came together beautifully with plank decks, forward hatch, main hatch, toe-rails, and bright trim. Note the teak cabin trim extending back around the cockpit.

We succeeded by bending thin pieces that were laminated together to form the proper curve. Though it was more work, we are extremely proud of it. It represents a problem faced and solved on good terms.

The bumper rails were installed temporarily, and the joints and edges fitted and sanded until everything fit. Finally, the wood was sealed and reinstalled with LifeCaulk and screws after the deck-hull joints were sealed.

After we set and fitted everything, we did the final finishing work, including patching, filling, sealing, sanding, and applying the required half-dozen coats of varnish. All the cedar was caulked with black polysulfide caulking and stained with desert sand–colored linseed oil stain/sealer, like the deck. The end result belies the deck's nasty condition just months before. It also preserved the traditional appearance. We were ecstatic with the results.

A week or so later, the caulk in the deck seams began separating from the deck planks in long, thin splits, and water filtered through. As the sun and rain worked the wood, more splits appeared. We covered the boat for the winter, but by spring the decks leaked like a sieve.

Localized patching didn't do any good, and the people at LifeCaulk offered excuses, but no help. Under their direction, we performed two strippings and reapplication of caulk (costing several $100 and a 100 hours of work), but the joints still failed.

I suspected that polysulfide is not compatible with white cedar and linseed oil-based sealer. We had no confidence we could do the caulking better, nor that it would change the outcome if we did. We hoped that being in the water might cure the problem. After all, a plank-and-caulk hull seals fine and it is built the same way. If the deck sealed after she was in the water, then we could do one more repair. So we decided to wait until she was launched to see what happened.

Nonetheless, the topsides were finished. They looked pretty good, but we had not yet learned that just because a wood structure works *under* water, it does not mean it will work *above* water.

> *After so many failures, the deck looked good,*
> *and it was done. That was what counted.*
> *But, we were wrong . . .*

8

SILENCE OF THE SEA, PART I: A BOAT WITH THE HEART OF A GOLF CART

A perfect morning. A magnificent sunrise on a flat sheen of water with just a touch of mist complements the warm cup of java tantalizing your nostrils and the barely audible feel of water lapping against the hull. Your ears sip the delicious sounds of the call of the seabirds tinkling across the water, an almost soundless splash of a bass snatching an insect, and just the whisper of a breeze.

Suddenly, all peacefulness is shattered by the roar of the engine. Insulted ears become abomination, as the smell of diesel blends with vibration of the sole and a cacophony of crew curses joins a raucously reverberating resonance in the interior. Such is the horror of most sailing mornings.

After a beautiful day of sailing, the anticipation of a perfect sunset in your favorite gunkhole is marred by the reverse scenario until the life of the offending mass of internal combustion equipment is gratefully extinguished.

We want to move a control lever forward to quietly ease up to our anchor, then glide off peacefully, with only sounds of wind, birds, and jumping fish to send us off.

We truly appreciate modern conveniences, such as electric lights, bilge pumps, and an auxiliary engine. My point is simple: We hate the noise, smell, expense, and maintenance of internal combustion engines. We hate fighting in and out of exposed gas-docks, unpredictable breakdowns, jury-rigged repairs in tiny spaces, or hanging off the stern in a seaway. To top it off, the engine had to come out to rebuild the hull.

In my 30 years of experience sailing different boats, the gas engine often ran at a noisy, smelly idle as we pulled away from, or nestled into, a slip. We had used electric trolling motors on boats for docking and we liked the silence and ease of use in tight quarters.

We felt that a properly designed electric drive would have enough speed and range for docking and maneuvering. It should also be suitable for gunkholing in short creeks and rivers of the bay as long as we had somewhere to recharge.

We wanted the security of two switched banks of batteries, so we could run one set all the way down and still have an equal amount of power available before we were "dead in the water," so to speak. Our calculations led us to believe we could travel for 6 to 12 hours with this setup without recharging that was about half the range most boats have with internal combustion engines.

We had no way of knowing for sure until we tried it out. We had already decided we wanted to sail, so the limited range and speed of an electric drive system posed no conceptual problem.

Should we change our way of sailing? We could discipline ourselves to sail long distances, or find a creek to gunkhole, or drop the hook and take a swim. We like sailing, and the auxiliary is really auxiliary.

We might not be able to adhere to a tight schedule, but a low-pressure style seemed attractive as we thought about it. What peace of mind had we sacrificed to the God of Modern Convenience and his evil sister, Internal Combustion?

The project almost died at the concept stage, since we could not find anything about the subject of electric drives, either in books, magazines, or from dealers. I was enthused about the concept of recharging batteries by using the electric motor as a generator when the boat was under sail. There are lots of examples, like windmills and towed generators, but we could not find any data on the subject.

The idea that the boat would be self-contained is simply elegant; as the wind drives the boat through the water, we would tap off excess energy

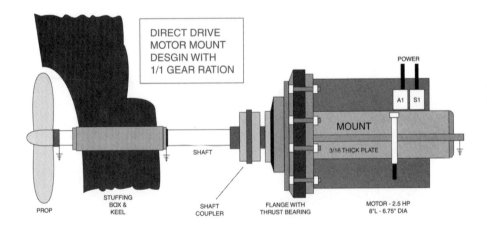

Our first electric drive system design has a 2.5-horsepower golf cart motor attached directly in-line to the propshaft and mounted in place of the original gas engine. Unfortunately, this was not nearly enough power to drive the boat properly.

through the propeller and store it in the batteries. Then we could silently tap stored wind power.

Our concerns were whether such a system would slow the boat down too much, and recharge her in an acceptable time frame. We felt that if we only used the system when we were already at hull speed, it would not be noticed.

We expected that we only needed an hour of power to leave and enter harbor, so we would have a full day of sailing to recharge it. With the right winds and sailing, it seemed we would rarely have to recharge the batteries, so *Rose* would be a wonderfully sound, ecologically sensitive vessel. She also would be quiet and odor-free, or did I mention that already?

We estimated that in a six-hour day of sailing, we would power perhaps 35 minutes in and out of harbor, approximately 10 percent of the time. There are days when we might gunkhole under power or run a channel or river canal for awhile. This would bring us up to 15 or 20 percent under power. The dockside charger would completely recharge both sets of batteries in one overnight session.

Was it too good to be true? We had a tough time finding the downside. Golf carts, fork lifts, car batteries, 100 years of electric U-boats, electric harbor boats, and taxis all gave credence to the idea.

But, if electric is okay, why doesn't everybody do it? If it's so easy, why don't boat builders offer it? Why don't we hear of it when boaters gather? We needed to know if such a system would work on a traditional sailboat. What about power and thrust? How long will the batteries last? Will the compass work? Can we get insurance? What is the dark secret that they are keeping from us? The Achilles' heel nobody talks about? Why the cloud of silence? It was not the bad things people said, it was the lack of anything said.

We read and talked to anybody who would listen. Though we received strange looks, as if we had dropped in from a distant planet, we never had any reaction other than a dubious, "Well, that's a neat idea. I don't know why it wouldn't work." We answered the doubts with research and we came up with a design. However, since our biggest problem was finding information, we made a promise to explain what we learned, so others wouldn't suffer through the same worries.

Skeptically, we began the conversion of a traditional gaff-rigged sloop to an electric auxiliary. We decided to experiment, with the commitment that we would back off and replace it with the rebuilt stinkpot if it failed. We even left the compartment intact, rather than convert it into locker space for the first season.

We bought a used golf cart from a supplier with a repair shop and parts department and did the conversion ourselves. Golf carts are proven technology, designed for weather and abuse. It seemed to have enough power and storage capacity for our needs and decades of performance on golf courses seemed to justify confidence in the design and components. All parts were cannibalized from this functioning cart.

The used golf cart also offered the advantage of off-the-shelf components that worked together to accomplish the job. The body and upholstery were poor, but the supplier checked out the mechanical and electrical components and replaced the batteries and cables, so the parts we needed were okay. We even drove around our yard for a week in our new toy before we tore it apart.

The estimated cost was about half the cost of a new internal combustion installation and comparable to a rebuild of our 37-year-old beast. It would weigh the same as the old gas engine, batteries, fuel tanks, and controls. Movable ballast would trim us, and more weight would be below the waterline to add to stability and handling.

The motor's small size frees up locker space aft. Controls tuck away in the cockpit, with fewer through-hull fittings, no explosive fuel, and no need to ever fight our way into a gas dock again.

We would "simply transplant" the drive train and control system, connect the propeller, and set up new control levers, right?

The design has the motor mounted to the flange, then to the thrust bearing, and then to a coupler that isolates the motor and propeller shaft from electrical currents and vibrations. Some customization was required, but that didn't seem intimidating until we started.

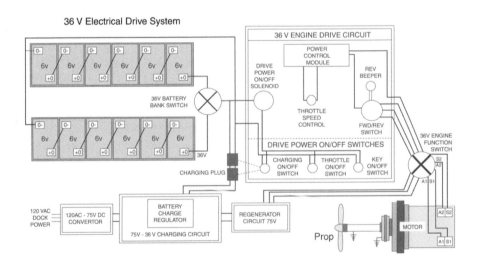

The propulsion system's 36-VDC electrical system is custom built, separate, and isolated from the utility 12-VDC system. In the future, we may upgrade to a 48-VDC system with additional 6-volt batteries or new 8-volt batteries to enhance drive.

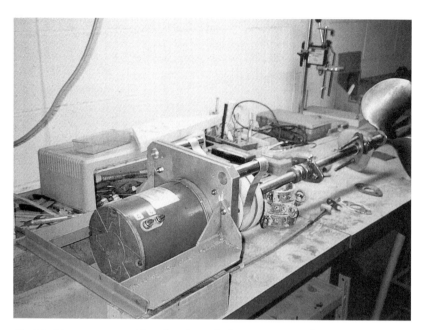

Electric drive system assembly and testing with the motor, mount, flange, and coupling attached to the prop-shaft stuffing box and propeller in the EDSL area of Rose's Dungeon. Cables, batteries, and controls are not attached.

As we pulled the motor, three unhappy facts surfaced: there was no front bearing on the shaft (it rode on a transmission bearing); there was no thrust bearing on the end of the armature (no thrust on the shaft); and it needed a lot of metal to dispose of heat (the aluminum transmission).

We had to manufacture a front flange/thrust bearing/heat dissipating assembly. The *simple transplant* took months of planning, shopping, machining, welding, finishing, and fitting. The aluminum flange was machined with fins to conduct heat away from the motor.

We tested one bank of batteries, cockpit mounted controls, and the 120-VAC dockside charger in the basement since the system could not be mounted until after launching. A big challenge was mounting a dozen 65-pound batteries (a total of 780 pounds) under the forward bunk so they would not move about in a heavy sea. We made allowance for strong battery boxes, spacious cable runs, and plenty of airflow to remove gas and odor when the batteries were charging.

A strong oak frame forms the top of each battery box, which fits under the berth. The area is vented from aft to forward, with the duct exiting into the dorade box in the forward hatch, so vapors leave the vessel.

I cannibalized professional jumper cables (#2) for 36-volt power from the battery banks. They run behind shelves and counters, along the port side to the cockpit, and carry electrical load while remaining cool, flexible, and well-insulated. These oversized wires minimize "hot spots" and run from one contact to another without splices.

We wanted the controls to be unobtrusive, so most electronics are hidden in the lazarette with the dockside charger. The golf cart wiring harness, cables, switches, and electronics modules were juggled around on an 18x18-inch plastic board to minimize the length of wires and the number of connections and to maximize neatness and reliability.

This board is mounted against the aft cockpit bulkhead inside the lazarette. The actual controls are on a small panel in the cockpit and the control shafts pass through the panel, the bulkhead, and the control board to activate the electronics.

In the cockpit, the control panel with on/off key, forward/reverse lever, and speed lever is mounted to the aft bulkhead, beneath the tiller. Silence is great, but operating clues are helpful for the pilot, so we added a green light when power was on and a blinking red for reverse (with intermittent beeper).

The drive shaft locks in a thrust bearing on the flange, which is bolted to the motor. The motor mounts bolt to the flange and to the wood beams where the gas engine was mounted. The assembly weighs 80 pounds and is 16x14 inches, compared to the 370-pound beast it replaced.

We found a larger propeller with three blades and more pitch that was far more powerful than the two-bladed prop that came with the boat. Because the new propeller was more efficient and powerful, it might also be strong enough to drive the regenerator. The disadvantage of the monster prop is the drag while sailing. This would hurt us all the time, but since we were less secure about the engine than the sailing, we decided to tolerate it as a starting strategy.

A missing element was the regenerator system. It *should* work, but nobody knew exactly what was needed. There is a problem: To push the boat, the propeller turns perhaps a 1,000 rpm, but it will turn only a few 100 rpm when it is pulled through the water at the same speed.

We decided to get the system working without a regenerator circuit, then measure performance, select a prop and gear ratios, design and build the circuit, and install it later. We've had bad experiences with electrical systems, but the history of the batteries, motor, and controls indicates they should be good for 5 to 10 years and they are easy to replace and maintain.

The challenge is contacts and terminators, which need periodic inspection, cleaning, and protective coating. But, that is the same situation with electrical connections in an internal combustion engine. We know that preventive maintenance is the best guarantee of fewer and less serious problems. I suspect we will be more attentive to these issues with an electrical-only system.

It took almost two years to get the pieces ready and tested in the basement Electric Drive System Laboratory (we called it EDSL, until we remembered the famous Ford car of that persuasion) workshop, otherwise known as *Rose*'s Electric Dungeon or RED for short.

> *These ideas, designs, and theories looked great,*
> *and we worked hard to build good stuff.*
> *But they had yet to meet the demands of reality.*

9

A *ROSE* IS A *ROSE* IS A *ROSE* . . . OR IS IT?

As we left the boatyard that first day, Cheryl said the derelict's name was *Bay Rose*—not that *she* would name her that, but that it *was* her name.

She described how it would have a beautiful transom nameplate in gold, with carved roses. Then we discovered that the plans showed nameplates under the bowsprit. Cheryl was ecstatic at the prospect of having three carved nameplates.

She apparently was ignoring the fact that I was not good at carving ham, much less wood. Anyhow, for the next six months all our attention, work, and money was focused on saving the boat. However, as soon as the hull was back in one piece, Cheryl insisted we work on the nameplates, so that the boat could be reincarnated. The cosmological principle could be debated, but I chose to tackle the work instead.

I had touched the carving tools as they came out of the box, but the skill to do anything creative with them was blatantly absent. I didn't even have a design yet. To buy time, I embarked on a planning effort.

I can design geometrically definable objects, but roses and nameplates are an artistic endeavor. I knew I was in way over my head with anything artistic, so I cheated. I scanned rose pictures and designs from magazines, books, and the Internet into the computer where I could doctor them up.

We found a white rose that Cheryl liked, but it lacked leaves (green stuff to make men feel guilty while eating meat). Searches of photos, books, Internet, and CD/ROMs yielded green, white, black, curved, straight, realistic, and stylized leaves. A day looking bought me one more day before I had to carve.

Perhaps it should be a red rose, instead of white. We could do more than one rose, along with vine-like edges (botanically incorrect for roses, but it looks kind of cool). We rejected everything, as the scanner worked overtime and the drawing programs started to seem like kaleidoscopic dream sequences—reaching for, but not quite touching—the perfect design.

Roses, roses, and more roses, snatched at the edges of my consciousness between moments focused on any subject. We churned out drawings: blossoms, clusters, baby roses, rose buds, giant bulbous roses, pink and white and red roses, all with foliage ranging from simple edges to great green bushes.

As Christmas approached, my desk was drowning in printouts, the computer was choking on gigabytes of roses, and Cheryl announced, "The boat doesn't like these. Let's go back to the original design."

It doesn't take a psychologist to predict the results: frustration, hurt, anger, and rage. Paper roses and designs strewn about in a temper tantrum, a mouse with its tail ripped out, and a keyboard with keys scurrying beneath the desk like ants at a picnic.

After months of messing with designs, I was on the verge of a nervous breakdown. With such an illness, I could spend the holidays in a quiet nuthouse with no computers, no scanners, no pictures, and God help anyone who brought roses to the patient.

But wives of 30 years have ways of dealing with spousal tantrums: the startled look, the pout, the hurt expression, and the cold shoulder. These techniques, refined over millennia, are designed to assert female innocence in the events, establish male guilt, and affirm the need for redemption for the offending husband. When things settle down, such a wife might even make a token concession so *all* the work was not wasted.

Miraculously, problems disappear like leaves that are blown off trees in a storm and then washed away by the rain. After a few days, the incident was not mentioned, the evidence disappeared, and things drifted back to normal. A bit later, the subject of nameplates came up and I was back on the job.

More work yielded a design with two ornate white roses on either side of the words "Bay Rose" to be carved into a block of wood about two inches thick. With final designs and Cheryl's approval, I embarked on manufacturing. Fearing more changes, I quickly started hacking up a piece of wood in the shape of the nameplates. However, Cheryl interrupted the work with a startling revelation, and she was quite pleased that she had solved a mystery.

She announced that the name *Bay Rose* was not right. She explained that the boat didn't like *Bay Rose,* and that was why we were having trouble with designs. Not only that, it was too long! With the final designs in my hands, she confirmed that the name was henceforth to be *Rose,* just one syllable and nothing more. Debate yielded only the response that *Rose* was her real name.

I admit to my naïveté when it comes to changing boat names, but I was beyond words. In self-defense, I put the wood and designs down exactly where they were and left them. I walked away without comment. Even a knockdown discussion later did not change my noncommittal attitude.

I did nothing on nameplates for weeks; pictures, designs, and wood blanks were stowed out of my mind. A rumor got around that I was on strike, though no statement was made to that effect. I tackled other projects, but even this backfired. When Cheryl saw the finished hatch boards, she noted that a rose should be carved into these boards as well. The rose project began anew.

I modified the designs to show the new name, resizing and reconfiguring so that everything was in balance and harmony again. I added the hatch designs, so now we had not one, not three, but *five* chunks of wood needing roses. I went through the scrapbook and stories I was compiling and changed every mention from *Bay Rose* to *Rose*. I saved everything, just in case.

The next set of designs was approved with little debate. I printed them on large labels and sized them to fit the transom, the bowsprit, and the hatch. I planned to make the real thing after I figured out how to do a name and a rose on a sacrificial hunk of wood (maple, rather than expensive mahogany).

An X-Acto knife cleared away the piece of label that would be cut with the router, leaving paper on the wood that would remain. To classify using

A dramatic curved transom nameplate with seven painted roses and brass letters. The custom transom light is centered above with vents on either side and the bilge pump outlets below.

the router as catastrophic would be understating the situation. A half-dozen attempts yielded mostly trashed wood and semideafness. The experience I gained eventually made me almost competent with the router, but the result was still unacceptable. Clearly, the router was a losing proposition as a carving tool.

I tried to create a rose with carving chisels. After two days and hours of work, I appraised the result. As I turned it over in my hand, exposing it to various lights and shadows, I smiled and congratulated myself for creating something artistic. With curves and delicate bevels, meticulously crafted edges, and precisely sanded surfaces, my rose looked suspiciously like a piece of tree fungus.

I proudly shared my artwork with my spouse and suggested we could rename the boat *Fungi* and we would have a nice carved emblem. She didn't appreciate the humor, so the carving task died, which halted the nameplate project.

The challenge was beyond me; the subtle colors and curves eluded me. I have drawn pictures for my mother with perfect perspective and been awed as she transformed my geometry into a creation of dazzling colors and textures. This project needed an artist and craftsman, and I was neither.

I tried a signmaker and an artist friend with no luck. A year and more had passed, and I didn't have any confidence that I could finish the first item on Cheryl's list: the nameplates she dreamed of as we left the boatyard that fateful morning.

God does have a way of handling things. In the fall of 1998, the rose project was reborn 3,000 miles away on a business vacation to England. We rented a canal boat to explore London and the Thames River while I taught a course. We were enchanted by a tradition of decorating canal boats with flowerpots, gardens, and stylized hand-painted flowers that were often

Nameplates with roses and inlaid gilded names fit on the hull and bow on both sides under the bowsprit. Each is made with two pieces on a hinge.

roses. These paintings (*not* carvings) are done with just a few bold strokes of even bolder color. Even better, the paintings are both attractive and doable with moderate skill and effort. We fell in love with their simplicity and attractiveness, though I admit my attachment may have been influenced by my desperation and their apparent feasibility.

We came home with dozens of photos and a new approach. Previous designs tried to show the glory of a rose, surrounded with leaves and vines. Each of many petals had multiple hues and layers to show depth, shading, and texture worthy of artists.

However, these canal boat roses were simple, with one or two colors and a few petals. They are painted on a flat surface, with no carving or relief. Each element was 10 times the size of an element in our old designs, giving us real hope. We even found rose decals as a starting point.

In my router experiments, I bought a pantograph advertising that anyone could create signs. With our canal boat designs, I could procrastinate no longer, so I retrieved the suspicious device and read the instructions. A large pattern is needed to make an object, since the machine reduces size by 50 percent and the tracer swings about 18 inches. For anything large, the wood and pattern must be moved and precisely repositioned several times.

Our designs were four feet long with no straight lines. It was back to the drawing board to create separate elements to make sure the positioning errors were less noticeable. With noise and luck, the router finally did its job, though it was probably the most expensive eight letters and trim in centuries.

The nameplates on the bow needed special mountings. The pointed tips fit under the bowsprit but had to be flush with the hull several feet behind the bow. This meant a very curved board, as on yachts, or two pieces like poor boats. Our two pieces could not be a fixed mount, yet they were firmly attached so they wouldn't pull loose. I designed an angled cut that laid the boards flush in three critical areas. They could be attached with screws, yet hinged at the joint so each piece supports the other. It worked perfectly.

The router cut edges as a frame for the artwork, but the letters were the scariest part. Even with the pantograph, the router tried to run off and destroy my work. Anyhow, I finished my job, sanded the blank, and prepared it with 10 coats of varnish.

Cheryl created stylized roses and plant matter with oil paints. It dried for weeks, then we finished it with six layers of varnish. They looked pretty good.

The nameplate on the transom was a puzzle. It curved in a nasty fashion, so we bent it out of thin plywood (1/8 inch) to match the transom. We aminated two pieces of thin plywood over the form, yielding a 1/4-inch-thick blank shaped to fit below the transom light and curve around the vents and drains.

The smaller center section of the nameplate was folded over that with two thin pieces of plywood, yielding a blank 1/2 inch thick and curved to match the transom.

We sanded the blank and finished with a dozen coats of varnish. Roses were painted onto thinner, outer sections on either side. We attached 5/16-inch-thick bronze letters with bolts from the back and through the thicker center section.

Roses are painted on the main hatch boards, which had been painstakingly restored using the original wood. If we look inside, we see rose-colored cushion covers, rose curtains, and even crew caps with *Rose* stenciled on them.

On our shakedown cruise, we added to the *Rose* couture with a cabin decoration and a small vase with a silk rose. Since then we completed the castle picture and rose bouquet paintings on the companionway panel.

Cheryl has a *Rose* flag for the stern flag post and one for the masthead flag halyard. I even heard her talking to the sailmaker about a giant rose on the jib. It is unlikely we can go much further, considering how far past outrageous we already are, but I'm along for the ride on such matters.

Experiments with designs and techniques lasted so long it was almost anticlimatic when we finished. The actual work was spread out over perhaps three months, but the 22 months of preparation wore heavily on us. Surprisingly, the final products look as if we knew what we were doing, and we show them with pride.

Soon *Rose* was rechristened, with appropriate libations to Neptune and all the ceremonies to rename a vessel. However, if we believe Cheryl, deep in her wooden soul, *Rose* was always *Rose*.

Our years with our Atkin sloop have proven that roses have many thorns, there is something fragile and beautiful about them that touches everyone, and *Rose* has touched all who shared her reincarnation.

We learned in a book that a famous painter
of canal boat designs lived in England
at the same time as the famous designer of our sloop.
Both were named John Atkin.

10

A COCKPIT REMADE

We all have an image of ourselves. I can see myself: tall, tan, robust, and in control of my destiny as I confidently steer toward the horizon, a firm hand on the tiller, while dashingly poised in the cockpit of a properly outfitted yacht. Since I am not tall, sport freckles, seem weak on the robustness, missed the dashing component when it was dispensed, and cannot afford a yacht, I pray for a nice cockpit.

The cockpit on a 25-foot sloop like *Rose* is the command center, pilot's station, helmsman's bridge, crew's base, and work area for lines and implements used for sailing, piloting, and navigating. It must handle four people as a living room, porch, and dining area for gunkholing and harbor activities. This is a big job for a space 5 feet, 8 inches long x 4 feet, 3 inches wide x 3 feet deep.

The cockpit in our backyard was not one I wanted to be seen in. During a 40-year life, it had deteriorated from use, abuse, bad repairs, design and layout problems, and poor judgment. Cleats, hooks, straps, screws, bolts, handles, controls, and instruments cluttered every surface already filled with leaks, cracks, and rotted sections. Teak trim on the cabin was not carried to cockpit coamings. Instruments, switches, and a variety of things were screwed into bulkheads (or hacked through) at random.

Plywood covered the floor (or sole in sailor talk), except for a 2-foot-long cut, through which protruded a steel bar welded as a gearshift handle. Water could easily pour through the crack to drown the engine, since tiny 1/2-inch throats assured debris could easily plug the two drains to flood the cockpit. A wide boom gallows blocked access to the aft deck, as it tried to hold up two booms at shoulder level, while it balanced precariously on top of two rusted pipes stuck in the deck.

A complete rebuild was the only option, but we wanted to comply with the designer's and builder's intentions and preserve the original wood when possible.

My self-image didn't include bird-headed tillers, but I was cajoled into saving it. Hours of work yielded a weird cross between the Philadelphia Eagles football team logo and the United States Postal Service trademark.

There were no flanges or drains around the seats, and I don't like to squish my butt around in puddles of cold water. These sensations did not fit my image, and neither did the rickety and weathered plywood seats, backs, and braces.

It was a tricky job, but we built new flanges and drains around the seats to control leaks into the lockers. These conduct water into U-shaped channels made from white cedar. Corners are sanded on a 1/4-inch radius, and joints are sealed to allow flex without cracking. To replace the creaky old seats, we found strong seats/hatches that do not flex under 200 pounds.

The cockpit floor was so badly mauled it could not be restored, so we built a new deck out of 1/2-inch white cedar over a plywood base, which fit over the original cockpit sole. This was nicely laid out with overlapping joints, framed edges, and trimmed with black joints.

Note the two 6-inch-diameter brass drains at the aft end of the cockpit, with a matching pair in the lockers. We can hose the cockpit and lockers down with little concern, but the safety of the vessel can be compromised by small drains.

In a worst-case scenario, what if the boat was pooped by a heavy sea or a knockdown? Though small (only 4x5 feet), the cockpit encloses over 20 cubic feet, which can hold 160 gallons of water, which could flood the lockers. The cockpit and lockers have a volume of over 60 cubic feet, about 500 gallons of water, in the wrong place.

Cockpit, stern, transom, and poop deck needed serious help. There was a lot of wood damage, as well as design and layout problems.

This scenario could put up to 3,000 pounds of water (half the vessel weight) several feet above and 10 feet aft of the center of buoyancy. Since capsizing or sinking would be bad for our self-image, we want to get rid of water quickly.

Four large drains exhaust below the waterline from 2-inch plastic pipes (*scuppers* in sailor talk). Large reverse flow valves prevent backflow in heavy seas or severe heeling and minimize gurgling, sucking, and slapping noises. This setup can drain several 100 gallons a minute from the aft section to aid recovery from a swamping problem.

The hard, plastic PVC lines are connected with rubber flex fittings that are double-clamped with stainless clamps. These should handle a great deal of stress and strain without leaking or breaking.

The cockpit is the center of sailing activities as well, so line placement is crucial. A major problem is the clutter caused by lines in and around the cockpit. Confusion and jammed lines may be the result of poor layout, and carelessness is often aggravated by poor design. The mainsheet runs down both sides of the poop deck, so it can be controlled from either side. It attaches to the end of the boom and a short traveler on the deck.

Both sides have blocks to mount winches and cleats to help keep the deck and cockpit clear. The two jib sheets run through blocks on the cabin trunk and then back to the winches. Halyards end on a teak block at the base of the mast and are controlled from the foredeck.

We needed cockpit stowage, so we emptied the cockpit lockers of everything except the emergency manual bilge pump (starboard) and the stove

A reworked cockpit with seat gutters, white cedar-planked sole, bronze drains, well-built seats, and instrument panels.

fuel tank (port side). This made room for oft-needed items, including the drink ice chest, to fortify ourselves in a hurry.

Confidence when sailing and navigating comes from information to help make the right decisions, but we could not find operable period instruments and controls. The type and size of instruments is always an issue, but just how many gauges can you fit, see, use, and more importantly, maintain?

We got rid of everything we could. The navigation station is the salon table, and the helmsman can yell any information the navigator needs. It sounds as if we stepped back into the Stone Age when I say it that way, but we survived years of sailing before we had electronics, and we remember enjoying it more, not less. In fact, I think our most pleasant sailing was when the onboard instrument was a tiny compass screwed onto the cockpit coaming.

Going electric was just the first step in our crusade for simplicity. We decided that we would survive with telltales and our own abilities to sense wind. However, with an average depth of less than 15 feet and thousands of square miles of shallow water, the Chesapeake Bay also sports shifting sandbars and tight gunkholes. There is no doubt that sailing the Bay requires a depth gauge.

Good navigation and sail trim is essential, so we added a boat speed/log indicator, a compass with a built-in heel indicator, barometer, and chronometer. The GPS and VHF are handheld models stowed in the cabin within arm's reach of the main hatch.

Though the instruments and propulsion system controls are quite modern, we wanted to preserve the traditional appearance wherever

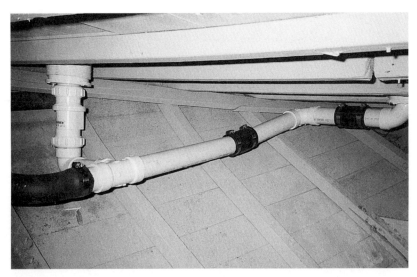

Powerful scupper systems assure that the cockpit and lockers drain properly, even if swamped. Each side has two large and heavily built drains with one-way valves. Double-clamped rubber joints permit disassembly.

possible. However, we could not find period instruments and controls that could be made operable. The nontraditional gauges and controls were painted black, then supplemented with brass trim that gave the cluster a more traditional look, and seemed to fit well with the designer's intentions. Small brass plaques were scribed with a simple design, while including labels and directions for every component. If possible, we used color-coding to make identification easier and more precise, especially in foul weather.

The backsides of the clusters are in accessible lockers in the cabin and lazarette, allowing maintenance and upgrades via a locker access panel. The thick dashboard mahogany was coated with six coats of varnish before the brass was installed and the edges were gilded with brass paint.

There are significant errors and sporadic failures of the instruments that may be explained as black magic by the electronics industry, but it does nothing for my confidence level. If we keep at it long enough, perhaps we will resolve these issues just in time for the instruments to be replaced with versions that are even more sensitive and failure-prone. That seems to be the way the electronics game is played.

Controls and instruments are mounted in dashboards; one is on the forward cockpit bulkhead (compass, knotmeter, and depth) and the other (engine controls) is on the aft cockpit bulkhead. The design is simple and elegant.

Each cluster was mounted into a 3/4-inch-thick rectangular, mahogany dashboard with 1-inch radius corners. We carved a simple groove an inch

The forward instrument panel houses a compass, depth sounder, depth alarm, knotmeter, depth alarm switch, and 12-VDC auxiliary power plugs. The cockpit fire extinguisher is close at hand, and two others are down below.

Aft motor control panel with speed (left side) lever and forward-reverse lever (right side), key switch, reverse sounder, and warning lights. The shore power (120 VAC) plug is visible on the left, and chargers are hidden.

from the edges, which were rounded to a 1/4-inch radius. The milling machine was used to carve openings for gauges and inlaid holes for switches and plugs.

A small lazarette hatch is positioned on the aft deck directly under the sweep of the tiller, so using it while under way could easily jam the tiller or break something. We stow the shore power cables there since they are used in the harbor. We built a new hatch to match the smaller cockpit, with a pleasant curve that was as much for strength as appearance. It easily supports the weight of a large man with no distortion, yet it weighs only six pounds.

We used white cedar planks on the hatch, seats, and cockpit sole, giving the aft section an integrated, planned feeling and traditional look.

The final touch is the mahogany main hatch with its decorative roses and varnish and the teak trim around the coamings, cabin, and hatchway to produce a planned appearance. As the cockpit took on an aura of respectability, a laminated wood tiller replaced the bird-headed tiller.

The boom gallows was moved farther back and made narrower to permit better access. Now we can sit on the aft deck directly behind the cockpit with greater height and visibility. In a turtleneck, I can even fake that dashing look from afar. It also seemed like a good place for wine and cheese, charts, and other stuff that fits the image.

On the aft end of the cockpit, the boom gallows and lazarette hatch integrate the cockpit with seating on the deck, while the massive rail on the transom complements the size and shape of the cockpit.

The end result gives no indication of the nasty condition the cockpit had been in just a few years before. By the end of our second shakedown cruise, we were satisfied that the cockpit was okay and only minor changes were justified.

Unfortunately, the deck leaked badly, and all attempts to cure it failed. Eventually, we covered the deck with cork, adjusted hardware, moved cleats, dropped two large and several smaller cleats, juggled the boom gallows further aft, and simplified line usage even further. The cockpit seemed quite comfortable in all regards except that I was exposed mercilessly to the elements.

Drowning is not as immediate as the prospect of frying under an August sun when the wind dies and temperatures scream past 90 degrees. A cockpit sunscreen is a useful weapon at such times, and it is more important than a life jacket most of the time.

I don't tan. My freckles run together to crowd out the charbroiled skin. I try sun protection, but an oversized body covered with white paste, followed a day later by zits and rashes, is not the image I prefer to convey. I sunburn whether I sail, power, anchor, or just sit at the dock.

I needed a sunscreen for all conditions. In addition, it should do no harm. It should not block access or vision, line-handling, or emergency responses. It should come down easily and quickly when it is not needed, and it should stow away nicely. It should not let the wind drag the boat around.

The final design is a single, flat sheet of material supported by three beams running from side to side. It is wider in the middle than on both ends to maximize coverage of the cockpit, and it tapers toward the ends to permit access from the decks.

Cheryl found a firm that makes a sun and weather-resistant material (Sun Fabric) that is attractive, soft, light, and strong, with an open weave to control light and air in greenhouses. This seemed perfect since air can flow through and it reduces, without blocking, all the sun. It permits some vision through the material (like a screen door), which seems practical for sailing. It was $28 and warranted for five years. Design was easier than creation, since I had to learn how to use a sewing machine. The idea is simple, but it seems that sewing machines were designed for people with some modicum of coordination.

Good times aside, I eventually sewed the cover together with doubled-over hems on all edges and a plastic-coated stainless cable in both ends to spread out pressure. Twelve 8x8-inch tabs were sewed in to hold the cross-beams, and then everything was checked out for size. It all fit!

I restitched the seams with one pass of heavy nylon thread for strength and wear. The edges were reinforced with plastic snaps around the critical points, and I placed brass eyes around the edges for lines and bungee cords.

We are proud of the cockpit and aft deck areas. Layout and line handling is safe and comfortable. Later, the plank decks were covered with cork.

To hold up the sunscreen, I made poles that were easy to use, quick to set up and take down, and solid enough to grab in an emergency. I used 1-inch-diameter dowels that were stained and varnished to blend in with the boat. These are topped off with a brass pin (a large screw seated down to the shaft, with the head rounded off). They feel good and look great poised in their bronze deck fittings; they also snap in and out easily.

The screen, its poles, and the lines roll into a light and easy-to-handle 6-foot-long package that fits nicely on the cabin top or stows above the berth. It is used hanging from the boom, self-supporting over the cockpit, or with the forward section folded over the aft section to cover the back half of the cockpit. The sunscreen can be covered by canvas to make a rain shield too. It can be hung from the main boom by central pelican hooks, which maximizes standing headroom. This positioning also permits it to be canted down on either side to block the late afternoon sun closer to the horizon.

In addition, the cover mounts on poles positioned around the front and sides of the cockpit, with the rear section over the boom gallows and behind the cockpit. The edges of the cover are then attached to the vessel with bungee cords and pelican hooks that assure it will not leave us unexpectedly. This setup looks nice and covers the cockpit well, while permitting easy access most of the time. It should work well under power or while sailing for a long time on a predictable tack.

The sunscreen looks just fine. The color, texture, varnished poles, and brass fittings give it a traditional look and it was very inexpensive (less than $50 with all the parts). A sunscreen is useful for most boats; it's easy to do, doesn't cost much, and it is rewarding because it's the perfect do-it-yourself boat project.

Handling charts in a small, heeled chaotic cockpit while sailing or in bad weather with a plethora of lines and the sweep of the tiller is tough. The top of the lazarette hatch is a key element in the resolution of such issues. Spring lines running diagonally across the hatch hold a clear plastic envelope that houses our chart book, markers, and gauges. This is all we need to handle piloting, and navigation can be done on the salon table.

The appearance of a clean, uncluttered design is apparent, and the cockpit and line operation were comfortable in our shakedown cruise. Several easy-to-use hooks and cleats helped with that comfort level. There are always opportunities to change things, and we are still messing about, but overall we are pleased with the cockpit. The basics are pretty good— kind of like we planned it that way.

We proudly stand in our cockpit.
I'm still missing the dashing component,
but the cockpit looks great!

11

A FIRST GALLEY

To sailors, about the only thing more important than the galley is the ice chest. Many believe you design the galley first, then build a boat around it. This idea gained credibility during the restoration.

Cheryl and I enjoy our meals (I carry around the proof), but *Rose* is a great Chesapeake Bay boat. Nowhere on the Bay is far from good restaurants, so starving is not one of our concerns.

We also enjoy gunkholing, so on occasions we pull out of the marina, find the nearest cove, and anchor for a day or two. We wanted a galley that would support such interludes, even in cold or damp weather, yet also let us head north to New England or south to Florida and sail in the open sea.

The confusing and congested interior layout was a mess when the boat adopted us. The galley seemed impractical because of poor accessibility and layout. There were two large counters aft, from under he bridge deck forward into the heart of the cabin, facing each other across the companionway ladder. One was immense (54x32 inches), with a large sink and built-in, front-loading ice-chest on starboard. The other was 42x32 inches with a large alcohol stove mounted atop the counter and a dry stowage area beneath on the port side. The lockers under the deck and behind each counter were almost inaccessible.

Stowage was accessible from doors that could not be opened when the ladder was in place. The space was over 3 feet deep, so a long arm was needed to reach any item in the back and anything stowed there would readily slide about as the boat heaved and heeled. This was not the galley of someone who sailed a lot.

A small counter/shelf spanned between the two along the aft section. There were 25 square feet of counter space, plus twice that in stowage. This is a huge space in a 25-foot boat, and I have sailed 45-footers without such galley space.

We ripped out the interior and the first question asked when guests saw the vacant space in her hull was "Where is the kitchen? Or whatever you call it?"

Our plan was to tuck a minigalley on the starboard side next to the ladder. We wanted the layout to seem as if it were originally designed to fit, with a traditional appearance. We felt a redesigned galley should be easy to use and compact.

We had to have built-in spaces for every item, including dishes, pots, and pans. However, let's face it, there is a strong gender preference in food selection.

I believe that foodstuffs are color-coded for safety and convenience. Many supposedly edible things (like vegetables) are coded green as a warning. "Do not touch: Reserved for animals!" Of course, man should then eat the animals.

Beyond tasty tidbits, some things are colored red or orange to sweeten our diets (apples and oranges). Odd-colored purple grapes and brown grains are destined to become wine and beer. Important boating foods (meat, fruit, and beer) should be cool, so I need an ice chest to load at the deli and fire for the steak before tearing it asunder.

Serious philosophy aside, Cheryl insisted on spaces for cereal, vegetables, and other barely edible stuff, as well as condiments, seasonings, dishes, utensils, pots, and pans.

AFT **OLD** **NEW** **FORWARD**

Original galley (left) was torn out and a new galley built (right) for more useful space and convenience in half the cabin space.

I tracked down a stainless sink and alcohol stove for very little money and designed the counter around these items. However, I could go no further without all the goodies, which I could not find from catalogs or over the phone.

I concocted a devilishly clever plan. I drove to my favorite marine supply house (50 miles away) and with only the help of three clerks and two customers, I picked out the perfect dishes and utensils for a wooden sailboat. I gave them to Cheryl as a Christmas present, and then I designed the galley around the dishes and implements.

In addition to fitting the dishes and implements, the galley was built in modular fashion; the pieces would fit through the hatch and could be assembled in the cabin before installation. The galley also needed room for hoses and electrical connections and to accomplish whatever might be needed. The final appearance had to be of an integrated and finished galley, so an incredible amount of time and energy went into messing about with designs and mockups to get it to look right.

One of the major guessing games was trying to gauge just how firmly objects had to be anchored in this boat. The last 25-footer I went out in had little ballast. It bounced and banged around, and sailed at 40-degree angles. Everything had to be tied down or else it was thrown violently about in the interior.

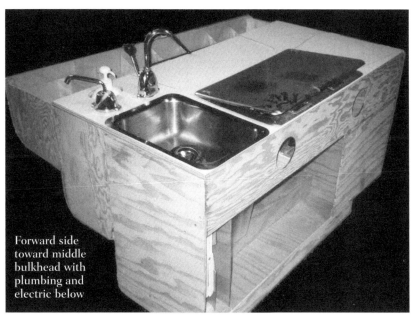

Forward side toward middle bulkhead with plumbing and electric below

The plumbing, countertop, and third module at the rear were completed after a trial fitting in the hull, accompanied by cursing and a lot of fiddling. The entire galley is shown pre-assembled for testing and planning before finishing.

On the other hand, some seagoing 32-footers I sailed could handle 5-foot waves without mauling occupants or equipment because they rode well and generally heeled only about 20 degrees in anything less than a hurricane.

We had never sailed *Rose,* but I expected she would ride well with her weight, ballast, and low-profile gaff rig. I suspected that the boat was not a voyager, but an extended weekender. If conditions got too rough in the Chesapeake, we would run for cover.

I set up the basic galley structure with only cabin measurements, the sink, and stove, but the third module needed careful fitting into the hull.

In hindsight, I guessed correctly. She is smooth, comfortable, and heels about 20 degrees while sailing. This was another case where a little luck is better than a lot of smarts.

The galley also had to fit in the boat, with space for hoses and electrical connections. The mockup sat in the basement as we dabbled with changes and redesigns, hoping to come to something that should work.

Note the three "steps" visible in the side view. Each "step" is the edge of a module that attaches to the others to form a complete galley unit. However, each module fits through the main hatch before we bolt it together. The open space in the "notch" is the channel for plumbing and wiring.

The stainless steel alcohol stove was in new condition. It worked fine, required five inches of depth in the countertop, and was almost flush when the top was down, so it maximized the use of the galley space.

We built the galley around the stove and found a sink to match it. The space on the aft end of the counter is the trash bin, which is 3 feet deep x 18 inches square. Its total of 7 cubic feet of space seems huge for a small boat, but there is never enough trash storage. It is lined with a plastic trashcan that holds a liner for a trash bag and can be removed for cleaning or repair work.

The Formica top was laid on 3/4-inch plywood, then hatches and inserts were cut out. It was easy to do once we found a truly flat surface and enough weights to hold it down while everything dried.

The third module is a custom-fitted dish storage area behind the counter. It is built of thin (1/8-inch) plywood that is tacked and glued together, then finished in epoxy and a white paint. It is open, so there are no hatches or doors to block access or air flow. However, the pockets are deep enough that nothing falls out or rolls around.

Cheryl is not tall, and I am left-handed while she is right-handed, so if I design something that works for me, she can't use it. She could not reach the condiments in the far corner of the galley, even when I tucked a step under the stove, so I promised to get that stuff for her and we ignore the nasty corner.

The galley storage capacity was about 5 cubic feet, and with two ice chests and other stowage, we could live a month on the food we could

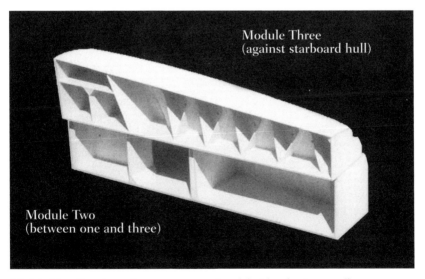

Module 2 has three large stowage spaces, and module 3 has fourteen small spaces shaped and sized for specific items. Each space is glued and fitted as part of a girderlike structure that only weighs a few pounds.

store. However, the water/liquid capacity is only five days, counting ice chests, and the 6-gallon water tank.

We avoided the issue of hot water with a boiling pot and a Sun Shower for personal use. We wanted outside water for washing and fresh water for cooking and drinking, so two hand-faucets feed the sink: one provides filtered outside water conducted by a high-volume unit, and the other provides water from the fresh-water tank, with a smaller pump to encourage conservation.

We hid a fluorescent fixture above the galley under the deck so we can see things inside stowage areas and in corners.

This was my first interior project, and the mockup sat in the basement for months as we dabbled with changes. Finally, we glued 1/4-inch and 3/16-inch marine plywood, with triangular braces on the joints, together so that it would be light yet strong. Screws were used to lock in the corners and other spots susceptible to strains. In some areas, the wood was so thin and fragile that I used small brass nails to hold pieces in place while the glue dried, but the glue was the actual structural fastener.

The job required dozens of clamps and jigs, a number of bungee cords, and some serious weights to keep the pressure on as the glue cured. Once the glue was dry, the structure was strong since it was composed of many boxlike structures that reinforced each other in a matrix. Though each of the modules was designed and built to handle stress while holding hundreds of pounds of appliances, food, and utensils, none weighed more than 50 pounds. The total galley (including sink and stove) weighed less than 150 pounds, empty.

The stainless stove and sink fit into the custom Formica top, and everything was light and elegant, attractive, and utilitarian.

A platform beneath the bridge deck hides two 12-volt utility system batteries, as the base for the ice chest. This large chest is portable, so we can load it elsewhere and carry it on board. It is well protected, double insulated, and opened infrequently. It holds things that must stay cold or frozen. During our shakedown cruise, we refreshed ice every few days and it kept everything frozen for three weeks.

A second ice chest in the starboard cockpit locker is accessible from the cockpit. It is opened more frequently and is more exposed and less insulated, to keep drinks cool.

The galley was finished in 1999, except for minor changes. It was my pride and joy, and it sat in *Rose*'s Dungeon for two years while the boat was being completed. I showed it to everyone and after they paid suitable homage, I released them to see other projects.

Alas, the fate of the galley was not in my hands. Unfortunately, all this hard work and design was later cast aside for a shiny bauble.

Sometimes we take things too seriously,
but children can lead us to a better perspective.
As I finished carving a gorgeous piece of teak with
the table saw and router, my two-year-old granddaughter
came down the basement steps with my wife, who asked,
"What is Pop-Pop doing?"
The answer sprang from the child's mouth:
"Pop-Pop is making lots of noise!"

ONBOARD UTILITIES

"Going electric" was one of those things that sounded easy, but became increasingly complex and intimidating as we thought about it. We already decided we wanted to sail, so the limited range and speed of the electric propulsion system seemed to pose no serious problem. It seemed such a cool idea, we wanted to give it try.

With enough research, we found answers that helped us get a design in mind. Then we had to turn those ideas into a safe, reliable, and functional electrical system. An earlier chapter discussed our electrical drive system, the first component of the overall electrical system. However, there were other issues, including 12-volt (12-VDC) power for lights, instruments, and bilge pumps, and the 120-volt alternating current (VAC) shore power system for battery chargers and tools while in harbor.

Fortunately, we found two sympathetic electrical engineers to help. Jeff Carstens understood electrical systems design, wiring, controls, regeneration, and related details. Bob Snow was the expert on corrosion and the dangers of electricity and metal in water.

The biggest problem was finding components and information, so we had to do a lot of research. The golf cart offered the advantage of off-the-shelf components that we knew all worked together to accomplish the job. In addition, we could simply transplant the drive train and power control system directly to the boat.

We installed the system without a regenerator circuit. We left plugs and space for the circuit to be finalized after we launched, when we could measure performance and experiment under various conditions. With real-world data, we could design and build the circuit, then install it later.

We did complicate the wiring with several more issues. What should we do about a 120-volt AC (VAC) electrical system? What do we do with the classic 12-VDC accessories usually used on a boat? What about the lights, the stereo system, bilge pumps, running lights, horns, air compressor for the inflatable, power plugs for computers, cell phone, and other 12-volt "necessities" of modern life?

The options were: set up a shared 12-volt system without batteries that borrowed 12 volts from the 36-volt batteries; set up a separate 12-volt system; or drop 12-volt accessories completely, converting the boat to 36-volt, including accessories. The shared option was selected for simplicity since we didn't have a clue where to find 36-volt accessories, and it was less expensive than two systems. This posed a problem of excessive drain on two batteries in each bank that provide 12 VDC, so we resolved to rotate the batteries each season to minimize differential use.

However, this design was not successful. We found that 36-VDC battery chargers cannot recharge all batteries in the bank properly if they are differentially discharged. We had to isolate the 36-VDC banks so they recharged as if they were one large battery, and all cells in the bank were always equivalent.

We opted for a separate utility system with two heavy-duty 12-VDC batteries mounted under the ice chest aft of the cabin area. We had already allocated this space for this function just in case the combined system was not the best choice, so it was not a major disaster when it didn't work. However, it did necessitate the addition of extra batteries, cables, wiring, switches, and automatic battery charger, at a cost of about $600.

The first challenge was the mechanical mounting of 14 batteries, weighing a total of 940 pounds. They almost fit under the forward bunk, until we made allowance for strong battery boxes, spacious cable runs, and plenty of airflow to remove gas and odor when the batteries were charging. We raised the berth 3 inches to make everything fit properly.

We didn't want batteries flying about the interior in a heavy sea, so the battery boxes were designed to handle loads in all directions. Each of the three forward boxes holds four 6-VDC batteries and are made from marine ply and fiberglass that is bolted to the crossbeams and mast step.

The top edges are fastened securely to the crossbeams that support the berth, while the leading and trailing faces are fastened to plywood bulkheads that run across the width of the boat. Each battery has a strap that passes through the box edge a few inches below the top, across the top of the battery, and through a similar hole on the opposite side.

The area is vented from aft to forward, with the duct exiting into the dorade box in the forward hatch, assuring that undesirable vapors leave. Power cables run along the port side, back to the controls in the cockpit, and are hidden behind the edge of the shelves and counters near the hull.

Each electrical system has a "floating" ground, so the ground or negative wires do not connect to the rest of the metal. This design minimizes the possibility of electrical current "leakage" and corrosion. Essentially, the system is isolated from everything in the boat by rubber and plastic insulators.

The drive system electronics wiring was not simple. The wires were labeled and the wiring harness was left intact when it was removed from the golf cart. Then it was positioned on a blank heavy plastic 5/8 inch thick and 18x20 inches (to fit through the lazarette hatch opening) board until the wiring arrangement was determined. After temporarily mounting the components, the wiring was experimented with until a layout was derived that minimized the lengths of wires and connections, and maximized neatness and reliability. Final drilling and milling was done for a professional job, wires were trimmed, and we fit the components in the final location.

Wires are high quality, oversized to minimize hot spots, and run in a single length from one contact to another. For battery cables, I used long, professional jumper cables (#2) with their clamps cut off. They carry the electrical load, while remaining flexible and well insulated. With a little luck and good maintenance, the electrical system should last as long as the boat.

We have had a lot of bad experience with electrical systems on board boats, and we researched the golf cart we cannibalized to maximize the lessons to be learned. The manufacturer's recommendations and operating history of the batteries indicate they should be good for 5 to 10 years before replacement, as long as they are stored with a charge and maintained at the proper fluid level. The real challenge is contacts, plugs, and terminators, which require periodic inspection, cleaning, and protective coating. Preventive maintenance is the best guarantee of fewer and less serious problems.

After feasibility, corrosion was a big issue. Dissimilar metals, like steel, bronze, and stainless steel corrode if they are in contact through a wet medium such as the wood below the waterline. The concern was how this phenomenon might be exacerbated by having 36 volts of electricity floating about the boat. Obviously, no matter how well we try to isolate and insulate, pathways will occur to let electricity flow some time or another. One remedy is to ground similar metals together and connect them to a zinc anode external to the hull. Since zinc will corrode faster than other metals, this tends to minimize damage to the metals we want to protect.

I was concerned with a dozen galvanized steel bolts that held the cross-beams to the keel. These bolts were still in decent shape after 40 years and

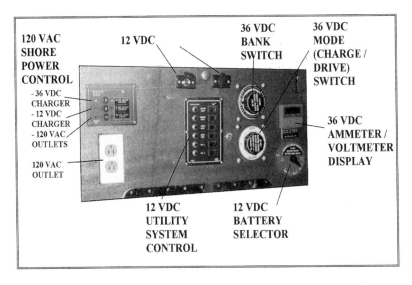

were essentially impossible to remove, so we were unable to replace them with stainless steel as we had with the other 100 bolts near the keel.

I had visions of our hard work falling apart after a few months as electrolysis ate important fasteners out of the hull, but our corrosion engineer assured me it was less of a problem than I had figured. We used three grounding circuits to minimize corrosion problems, which was still a touch of overkill. The power system and controls "float" with no external ground, completely isolated from everything else. The motor itself is grounded to a through-hull zinc anode nearby, and the prop and shaft have a zinc anode on the shaft directly in front of the prop.

Stainless straps on ribs and crossbeams are connected with a stainless rod grounded to a zinc anode, so they do not interact with all of the bronze, lead, and galvanized bolts that we could not remove from the crossbeams.

Our expert did point out that *nothing* will stop electrolysis and corrosion, but we can minimize it with design and preventive maintenance.

Our next challenge was mounting the engine properly, and what seemed a simple mechanical task actually turned out to be a complex engineering feat.

We wanted the electric drive controls to be unobtrusive. We settled on a simple control panel with an on/off key, a forward/reverse lever, and a speed lever. It is mounted to the aft cockpit bulkhead against the lazarette with the controls conveniently out of the way beneath the tiller. The dockside recharger is easily accessible with the hatch open.

Going all electric was just the first step in our crusade for simplicity. The forward panel backs up into the main electrical panel under the companionway, whereas the aft engine control panel backs up into the 36-VDC electric-motor control board in the lazarette with the 36-VDC charger system. Except for the batteries, almost all components of the electrical system are accessible either through the lazarette or directly below the main hatch. The electrical system has an ammeter to show charge rate and a voltmeter to show battery condition.

The electrical system was challenging enough, but the ultimate bugaboo to me was the plumbing. I'm amazed how much plumbing there is on a boat. There are inlets, outlets, scuppers, drains, tanks, fuel lines, bilge pumps, emergency pumps, vents, and more. The whole idea is a bit of a conceptual challenge for me. When we started to save *Rose*, I worked hard sealing the wood hull to keep water *out* of the boat.

When I was done, with no leaks, I had to punch a bunch of holes through the hull so we can let water into the boat. Then for more of a twist, we have to punch other holes in the boat so we can pump the water back out again.

I designed a nice-looking plumbing plan, but what looks good on paper looked much worse in reality. No matter how many times I messed around to make the plumbing look neat and orderly, it seemed to resemble a rat's nest of tubes and fittings. I couldn't find a friend or family member to volunteer and no plumber would even discuss it, so it was all mine.

Though this was a restoration, it should come as no surprise that for the plumbing I did not follow accurate restoration. I used plastic with great abandon. In any case, lead is illegal, and I can't solder bronze worth a damn. The heat gun turned out to be a critical tool for plastic hoses. First off, the diameter of the hose on the inside is usually far less than the diameter of its fittings. By heating the hose, then pushing and cursing belligerently, some of them can be intimidated into fitting onto the coupling. This may take several attempts before the stupid chunk of plastic understands that you intend to win, so it better give up soon. I found that taking a utility knife violently to the offending chunk of plastic, hacking and whacking it with lots of sound effects, seems to work well. At times, I was heard cursing as my fingers cooled from a roasting while jamming hoses onto a too-large fitting with the heat gun. These were topped off with double clamps on lines that connected to through-hull fittings below the waterline.

I was concerned with the corrugated hoses since they are so light and thin. Then one day I accidentally cut one while rerouting a wire to the electrical control panel. It seemed that if it cut so easily (by accident) that it was just a matter of time before it tried sinking us. That afternoon, I bought 20 feet of heavy, smooth bore hose and replaced all the exhaust hose below the waterline.

Finally, I fitted the head floor and new toilet. I jammed the really nice outboard counter into the tiny space and finished the cabinetry. We were shocked how much stuff we were able to jam into a tiny space. With the addition of a simple partition between the companionway and the toilet

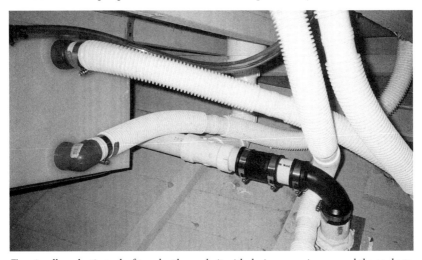

Two 6-gallon plastic tanks fit under the cockpit with drains wrapping around the tanks to through-hull fittings. The sewage system with a holding tank is complex, but necessary, to sail offshore and enjoy the Chesapeake Bay. The tanks straddle the motor with a heat shield. All plastic hose shown here was replaced later with much heavier hose and dual clamps on each joint.

area, the portside interior materialized. We dragged friends and relatives into the bowels of the boat to check out the fitted toilet. They humored us, but toilet testing was pushing it. They smiled and slipped back to the safety of the cockpit.

The fresh water and sewage tanks fit in the engine compartment space too, but suspending tanks under the cockpit was a tough job since they had no mountings, but lots of right angles. I resorted to a combination of straps and oak braces reaching across the hull to finally trap them where they wouldn't break loose.

In my naïveté, I looked for two different sizes of hoses and fittings; a small size for inlet and a large for outlet stuff. However, none of the utensils, tanks, or valve fittings are the same size. The external water supply system has a through-hull fitting that connects to a filter, then lines to the galley sink pump and the head inlet pump. The internal water supply system has a deck fill and lines to the tank, then a vent from the tank to the transom, then a line from the tank to the galley sink pump.

The waste-water system has a line from the head to the waste tank, a vent line from the tank to the transom, then a line from the tank to a valve to switch between external exhaust or the pump-out line, which then goes to a deck pump-out fitting. The galley sink has a drain from the sink to the exhaust. Every pump, faucet, and valve is some other size than the pipe, hose, or fittings. There are different-sized screw fittings, and then there are different sizes of threads on the same size fittings; it was a nightmare of ill-fitting parts.

Double clamps on each fitting are proper, but I violated this at times since only divine intervention could get the plastic over the fitting—there was no possibility it would come off, even with one clamp. However, I did put double clamps on all lines that connected to through-hull fitting at every point below the waterline as insurance.

It is hard to get excited about electrical systems until they don't work.

Though not very rewarding as a project, plumbing must be perfect.

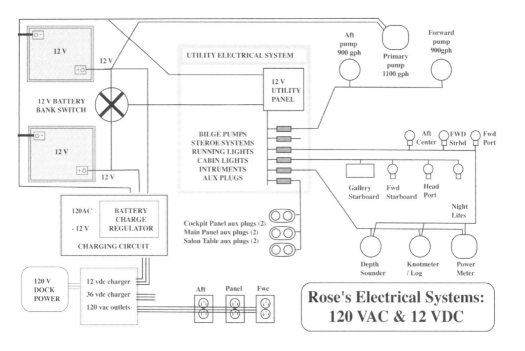

Rose's Electrical Systems: 120 VAC & 12 VDC

Electrical System Design. Three independent electrical systems (12 VDC, 36 VDC, and 120 VAC) are controlled at a single control panel. They interconnect at the 120-VAC shore power, which automatically charges twelve 6-volt batteries in the 36-VDC drive system and two 12-volt batteries in the 12-VDC utility system.

13

ON FIRE AND FOOD

A bear has its den, a bird has its nest, and man has a hearth. We pride ourselves on an image that gathers together the ideas of fire and food into a key element of man's world. We define ourselves in terms of our hearth's size, design, and cost. When we go to sea, we carry our hearth with us.

I like eating and being warm, a fact that we tried to address in the redesigned and flexible interior. I endure comments about the food I ingest, and sermons on the evils of sugar and cholesterol. I tolerate ribbing about turtlenecks, sweaters, and the tropical heat inside my winter home.

We jammed a lot of living space into a small vessel with the berth at the front, the salon amidships, and a comfortable galley fitted under the starboard aft quarter.

Alas, the fate of my galley was not in my hands. It began innocently at a flea market, where a dulled brass texture caught my eye. Examination revealed 80 pounds of noble metal machined to

A Taylor bronze two-burner stove with oven, grill, and lots of stuff, such as cast-iron burner caps, air and fuel lines, pressure gauge, air pressure pump, and pressurized fuel tank. Note the bronze rails around the top.

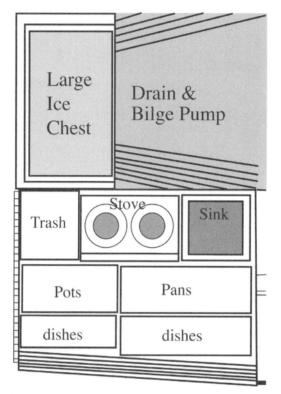

boil a teapot, cook crumpets, and warm a cabin, all at the same time.

The Taylor Model 030 stove/oven/heater is a British contraption that burns kerosene. Brass rails encircled a glazed but chipped cast iron counter with round inserts and louvered holes for warm air to flow to the cabin. Three kerosene burners, a brass pump, pressure gauge, and tank verified this as a terribly British piece of galley equipment.

The most obvious problem with the stove was the slight matter of my wonderful galley that I had built and

The plan for the second galley was basically the same as for the first, but the stove was a different size, so the front module of the galley changed dramatically. The back two stowage modules stayed close to the same design.

planned to install the next weekend. Desperately, I convinced Cheryl the monster was overweight, inconvenient, and not worth $550, so we left it there. However, Cheryl's infatuation got the best of her and when we got home she called to make a lower offer on the item, which the owner accepted. The next day, Cheryl called the "owner," who told her they were open until seven o'clock, that they could not ship it, and that they did not accept credit cards. Undeterred, Cheryl begged our daughter Jennifer, who lived closer to Annapolis, to drive over with her emergency cash to get the beast for us.

Jen had plans that did not include a trip to Annapolis, especially on boat show weekend. Late on a busy day, she rushed into rain-swept and crowded Annapolis, got stuck in traffic, and found the place closed.

She was not the happiest daughter on earth when she called. The owner was tracked down and disarmed by the onslaught of Cheryl and Jennifer. He graciously drove back to the warehouse and reopened to give the stove to Jennifer. He pointed out that he would have happily shipped the stove to us and put it on a credit card. At that point, my sweet daughter shared many foul words (which I like to pretend she does not know) over FCC-regulated phone lines. As if its acquisition was not ominous enough, it took months to get the stove running and then it failed, demanding frequent rebuilds and hassles. It

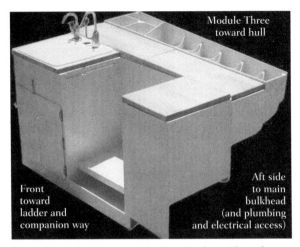

Module Three toward hull

Front toward ladder and companion way

Aft side to main bulkhead (and plumbing and electrical access)

The galley with all three modules from the front. The sink is on the left, with a large open space for the gimbaled stove in the center, and the trash on the right. There is stowage beneath the stove and in the back two modules.

always looked great, but it never worked worth a darn. But that was not even the worst of it.

To use this monstrosity, we needed a new custom galley. With a tear in my eye for the hard work and ingenuity I was about to destroy, I hacked the completed galley to pieces, tossed aside the planning and design, ripped out the carefully structured corners, shelves, facades, and well-crafted components. I retained one module and the structural supports that fit the hull; then I started over.

Because the top of the beast was smaller than the previous stove, I expanded the counter. Yet, the height was radically different and I had to cannibalize the dry storage space to accommodate it.

To make it even more challenging, the new external kerosene system called for plumbing to be manufactured and installed.

The stove has a deck fill, a fill line, the tank, a pressurization line from the galley area, and a fuel line to the galley, along with fittings, pumps, valves, vents, and pressure gauge.

All of the lines could not be plastic. The pressurized kerosene stove needed pressure-fitted copper lines and brass fittings. The fuel tank in the starboard cockpit locker feeds fuel through the filter and the bulkhead into the stove inside the cabin. The hand pressure pump is also in the galley.

It has a deck fuel fill and line, a pressurization line from the galley area, and a fuel line to the galley, along with a filter, fittings, hand pump, valves, vents, regulator valve, and pressure gauge. The copper and brass fittings leaked and were redone dozens of times before we finally sealed them. Somehow, we did manage to get the stove working, but it was an uneasy

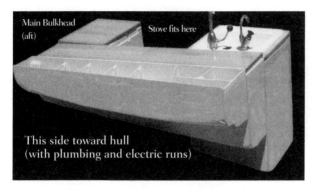

The assembled galley modules before installation, so we can see how they will fit into the curve of the hull. The notched areas beneath each module are spaces for plumbing and wiring to run along the inside of the hull.

relationship from the beginning. A big problem is getting the burners started with an unwieldy propane torch, which is undependable and a lot of work. Once it is going, the stove is adequate and even neat.

Of course, the brass stove could not share counter space with a stainless sink, so the unused sink was replaced with a new sandstone sink with two bronze hand pumps to provide water from outside or from a 6-gallon fresh water tank.

My custom designed and hand-built Formica countertop was replaced with Butcher-block tops that provide access to the stowage and even the trash bin in the corner. The new sink fit perfectly into the custom top,

and the back two modules were retained with only minor changes from my first design.

The stove is gimbaled, but its movement is restricted to about 20 degrees, enough to swing at anchor. Though not for around-the-world cruising, it is fine for Chesapeake Bay weekends. A moderate angle made construction simpler and saved space.

Marine plywood of 3/8- and 5/16-inch thicknesses with triangular braces on the joints was glued together to form the structure in the front two modules. The plywood and braces were heavier than the original modules, but light and strong, and also yielded minimal space to the structure. Screws were used to lock in the corners and other spots that were susceptible to strains.

In some areas, the wood was so fragile that I used small brass nails to hold pieces while the glue dried, but the glue was the primary structural fastener. The job required dozens of clamps and jigs, bungee cords, and serious weights to keep the pressure on everything as the glue cured.

Once the glue was dry, the structure was strong since it was composed of many boxlike structures and pieces that reinforced each other in a matrix. Though each module was designed and built to handle lots of stress, none of them weighed more than 50 pounds. The total galley weighed less than 250 pounds empty, and one-third of that weight was the stove. When we were done, less than half of the galley resembled its first incarnation, and the plumbing, locker, and bulkhead design had undergone changes.

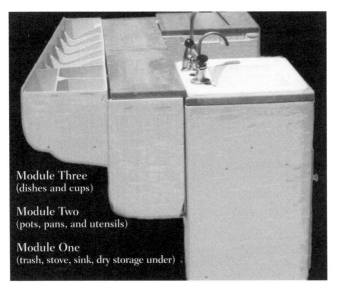

Inside the image:
Module Three
(dishes and cups)

Module Two
(pots, pans, and utensils)

Module One
(trash, stove, sink, dry storage under)

Galley from the side: Cabinets taper toward the back with plumbing below, the hull is to left of view, and open space in the cabin and the ladder to the right. Bottom: Side toward bow with all three modules.

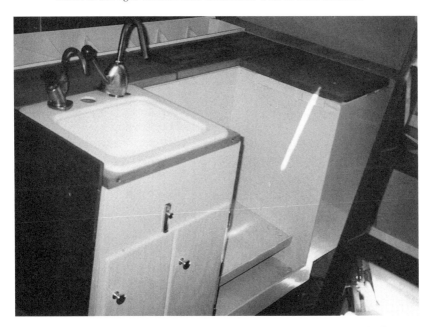

Looking aft and starboard at the galley with sink, stove, and trash bin across the front. Two bronze water pumps provide water for the sink, and the pressure gauge and air pump for the stove's pressurized kerosene are visible next to the fire extinguisher on the bulkhead. Final teak trim rails across the front are not in place, so we can see construction details.

My warmth-seeking activities came to no good when we tested the stove in the basement. The burner joints leaked pressurized kerosene, which ignited into a four-foot torch. The flames arched up and across the basement timbers and scorched the underside of the floor. Three burner rebuilds stabilized the tendency toward self-immolation but left us feeling queasy about its use in a wood boat.

We found a repair shop on the West Coast that could rebuild our burners. This group, A&H Enterprises in Tustin, California, was very nice, and their enthusiasm was refreshing. Once the tank, stove, plumbing, and all parts were checked out, the mockup was disassembled in the basement and packed into the station wagon to be installed on board.

They sent instructions of how to use it, which I had engraved on a brass plate and attached over the pressure system on the aft cabin bulkhead. After a few hours of training, almost anyone with a degree in rocket science can light the beast.

The back of the stove gets hot, so surrounding wood is faced with brass sheets to protect it from the heat. A metal pocket along the backside holds implements, and there is room for the flexible fuel line to connect the gimbaled stove to the pressurized fuel tank in the cockpit locker. The brass sheets are trimmed to fit around the openings with a vent in the back for access to plumbing. The hand pump came with the stove and is solid brass, so fittings were found to maintain the brass-engineered look.

The starboard cockpit locker has the pressurized kerosene tank, fuel lines, and filter. The tank is filled from a bronze deck fitting outside the cockpit. It has a pressurization line from the galley area and a fuel line to the galley, along with a filter, fittings, hand pump, valves, vents, regulator valve, and pressure gauge. It holds 25 pounds per square inch of pressure, and the copper and brass fittings leaked and were redone dozens of times before sealing. However, despite our efforts, we cannot use more than one burner at a time. It seems that the heat causes pressure oscillations that blow the flame out.

Each module was designed to fit through the main hatch, but in the process of modifications, the weight increased so much they were hard to handle. It took hours to get the pieces lined up and mounted. Excess weight also strained the brackets, so #8 screws were replaced with twice as many 1/4-inch through-bolts before I was satisfied that parts would not shift in hard sailing. With the extra weight and stress factors, it was a guessing game trying to gauge how firmly objects had to be anchored.

As I've previously explained, we had never sailed *Rose* before, and we didn't have a clue how she rode. Intuitively, she should ride well with her heavy weight, ballast, and her low-profile gaff rig. But since we didn't know, each decision was fraught with uncertainty. We were not using the boat as a voyager, but as an extended weekender in the Chesapeake. If things got too rough, we would run for cover, but *Rose* is smooth and only heels about 20 degrees while sailing intelligently. We got lucky this time.

Our mockups worked well, but the changes for the stove and the higher rail placed the far corners in the back of the galley out of Cheryl's reach. It took a bit of compromise, but I agreed to reach anything lost in the back of the galley. A fluorescent fixture over the galley sheds light in each corner and crevice, backed up by mellow cabin lights and an oil lantern. Heat buildup in the galley area is eased by two portholes, a vent, and the main hatch, which is generally open.

A step-up platform beneath the bridge deck provides space for the two 12-volt utility electrical system batteries, as well as a base for a large ice chest we load elsewhere and carry on board. This ice chest is well protected, double–insulated, and opened infrequently. It holds things that must stay cold, and we have had it keep shrimp frozen for up to three days without refilling.

After all that, *Rose*'s galley was again complete with sink, stove, ice chest, lots of wood, and brass. It is spacious and comfortable; it feeds us and keeps us warm. What more can you ask?

> *The galley is so unique that everyone is distracted by it,*
> *so they don't talk about my eating and dressing habits.*

14

THE CENTER OF THE WORLD:
A SALON

Cheryl's rescued hulk had nowhere on the inside to sit down and partake of good companionship over a cup of tea. We wanted the largest dinette we could squeeze in, with a solid and attractive table that was removable and could fold down to a minimal profile.

We built in two settees facing each other amidships that butt up against the berth. The cushions for the settees and berth had to be right.

There are some projects under the protection of the softer gender. These are issues of such high emotive sensitivity and artistic flair, they cannot be entrusted to males. For items such as colors and patterns, I defer to Cheryl, and this policy contributes to the longevity of our marriage. I have strong opinions of what I like or don't like. But, they are put to better use when those opinions are not voiced.

Cheryl ordered cushions for the berth and two settees with a fleur-de-lis pattern. It matches the richness of the wood ceilings and interior trim. The backs of the cushions have a strong netlike material, so air can help to keep the foam dry. The cushions put a heck of a dent in the budget for the boat project.

The berth cushions were 38 inches wide, too wide to move around or through the hatch, so we cut a triangular piece of foam (14x30 inches) on the corner of each berth cushion to make them easier to handle. Since water instantly soaked into the foam, we got closed cell foam and doubled the cost to about $800.

With a usable salon, we now needed a nice table with access to the settees with the leaves up or down. I built a frame around two legs that fit into fittings under the floorboards and are anchored by a pin to the bulkhead across the berth at the front of the dinette. The table leaves fold down on either side of the legs, but are still rigid enough that we can bump it or hang onto it without breaking or twisting it, even in a seaway.

When the leaves are down, a small shelf remains on the top of the legs, framed by a lip formed by the leaves, and wide enough to set tea cups and coffee mugs. The reduced size of the table acts as a small cocktail table between the settees.

I had to shorten the table legs by a 1/2 inch and the length by an inch to fit it through the main hatch. Corners were trimmed so a body can squeeze into the settee when the leaves are in raised position. The leaves were trimmed by an inch to let them open without jamming on the cushions. The engineering and ergonomics of the table took more time than the construction, and the construction took far more time than I imagined.

We used teak to match the flooring; we wanted all the materials to fit together in the interior. The 5/8-inch teak and holly plywood is the same material used for the rugged floorboards.

One problem was making the frame strong and straight, square and level, and perfectly rigid. My son-in-law convinced me that this could only be done with a mortised joint. I blanched at the thought of another tool, even one that drills square holes.

We cut ends of the crossbeams into rectangular sections, then embedded them into holes drilled into the square leg by the mortiser. Careful use of these joints, many clamps, and plentiful amounts of epoxy bonded the legs and crossbeams into an extremely strong frame. The frame uses an extra support strut on the leaves, making them more rigid, and anchoring the supports on two turning arms locked to the frame.

The force of a human body on the table or falling across the cabin in a seaway is significant. I reinforced the leaves for strength three ways:

Roses's Salon Table Design

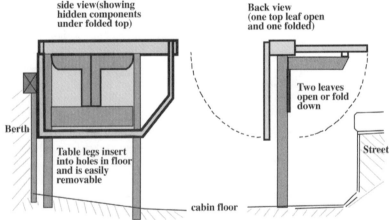

The centerpiece of the salon: two settees for four adults frame a movable teak table with two folding leaves and room for four dinner settings or a party.

• long piano hinges are well attached into the leaf to assure plenty of rigidity at the hinge joint;

• attractive fiddle edges are teak braces, epoxied and screwed into the edge of the plywood, and finished to look good while adding strength; and

• a brace below the leaf that presses on a longitudinal brace running the length of the leaf, which spreads pressure from the support brace.

There is some flex when a great deal of force is put on the leaf, but it firms up quickly and supports a lot of weight without feeling as if it will break or split. This is backed up by a substantial brace below the floorboards, screwed into the massive keel for the two legs and a matching brace on the amidships bulkhead, to hold the forward upright leg in place.

Another major task was trimming the fiddle edges of the leaves. The edges had to cap the plywood; protrude up slightly to keep plates and utensils on the surface when the boat was rocking; and support elbows, leaning, or anything thrown against them. They had to be attractive, yet strong enough to handle the human bodies that people jammed in and out of the cabin, berth, and settees.

Teak trim measuring 1/2x1 inch with rounded edges was screwed and glued to the plywood on the outside edges of the leaves. Since they are partially hidden and free of wear, the inside leaf edges near the center are 1/8x1/2-inch strips.

The two large caps on the shelf hinge area in the center are also teak, and they cover the edges of the shelf and the hinges on the leaves. They also act

In the down position, the edges of the leaves frame a convenient 4-inch-wide cocktail table and shelf surface with a 2-inch lip for storage and a very strong handhold.

as the fore and aft lip on the shelf when the leaves are down. Two massive edge caps were carved using the belt sander, Dremel, and hand chisels.

I mocked up other projects to check for fit and appearance as I went along. However, because of the design, I could not assemble the table ahead of time. Suddenly the pieces converged into the same place at the same time and it was there, looking like my scratches on paper had predicted.

It shocked me to a new level of awareness in my growth as a carpenter. It was a drawing converted into an object without growing in slow steps along the way. It was a marvelous moment of self-actualization.

All relevant insights aside, the table reached the stage where each little job improved its appearance dramatically. One aggravation in life is that nobody notices 10 hours of sanding to get the surface right, but everyone reacts well to the first coat of varnish, which takes about 15 minutes.

This project was my first attempt at furniture building, and I am not proud of the mistakes I made along the way. For example, the miter saw broke a sliver of wood off the most visible corner of the trim (I discovered later that some paper tape over the joints before cutting can prevent such damage.)

I learned that carving with a chisel often is the only way to do a job, but there are requirements for success: sharp chisels (not just sharp, but *sharp*), good light (so you can see surfaces), good clamping (firmly anchored), and patience (slow and easy). I wasted a lot of time and teak redoing things, and it took a lot of filler, sanding, and repair work to cover up the worst of the damage. From a distance it is okay, but on close inspection the repair work is somewhat amateur.

The flooring is an important part of the salon. Not only is it made from wood like the tabletop, but it is trimmed to match with white lines directly over each other. The idea was that the extra complexity of the lines in a small interior would be more acceptable if they lined up. It worked like a charm. However, the floorboards were nastier than I expected. First off, the holly- and teak-veneered plywood cost a small fortune, so I was afraid to cut it up or to stand on it while I restored the boat. I made floorboards of rough plywood to use until restoration was done, while the nice plywood waited three years.

Long before I reached that stage, I noticed a serious issue. The rough floorboards refused to fit and they had weird features. I trimmed them smaller, but then they just flopped around. I put shims under them, but that caused gaps. The boards were temporary, but these gaps had amazing qualities. Anything that I dropped found a gap and squirmed through it to hide deep in the bilges. Statistically, the gaps are about 1 percent of the surface. Why didn't 99 percent of dropped items land on top?

This was an oddity, but as the offenses grew, I lost patience. I put duct tape over the gaps, but the dropped component would scurry about my feet until it found a tiny opening, then hop through into the bilges. This observation graduated into an obsession. I trimmed and re-cut the floorboards, overlapping a floorboard awkwardly over the largest offending gap to assure no possibility that anything could sneak through.

The problem got worse and the sounds of my voice echoing across the backyard, bellowing epithets, was embarrassing. I had to do something about it. After three years of escalating warfare, I surrendered. I bought tools in large quantities, i.e., one for the job, one to toss overboard for Neptune, and one to offer to the gods of floorboard joints. Of course, there was also the standard extra needed for every job that feeds the toolbox monster.

I feel better now, and I haven't had any floorboard fits lately. However, when the ballast has to be pulled out again, we will find the boat has gained hundreds of pounds in brass screws, nails, pins, and hardware, but I will deal with that later.

After the boat was in the harbor I cut and trimmed the final boards to fit, using the junk floorboards as templates, and added a coat of varnish to seal them well. I positioned them and trimmed away edges to accommodate bolts and joints until they fit and laid flat. I drilled large holes so they could be removed easily with a finger and water would drain swiftly, and sealed them again before I left for the night. The next day, I discovered that a sliver of wood from my previous day's trimming exercise had jammed the bilge pump, and the floorboards were floating in 10 inches of bilge water. The soaking revealed that the expensive plywood delaminated in the water.

What a perfect choice for floorboards; I could hardly believe that it was not marine grade, but I couldn't return it. Flustered, I dragged the mess home and dried the boards while clamping them so they would delaminate and warp as little as possible. We impregnated the layers with epoxy, then clamped it together, to create our own marine plywood. When fixed, we sealed them with epoxy, varnish, and a sprinkling of sand for a nonskid surface.

I also created a teak grate between the ladder steps to collect water to the bilge pump. A feature of this setup is that the main hatch acts as a stall for the Sun Shower hanging from the boom and drains through the grate to the bilge.

This is a great grate, and it was easier to make than it appears. The wood was trimmed to 3/4 inch square and cut into lengths. Then it was clamped together and drilled for three long, brass-threaded rods from side to side. As the rods were treaded through, pieces were epoxied to each other, then clamped, and the rods were tightened. After the epoxy set, clamps were removed and the grate was ready for painting and nonskid sand. It looks a lot better than the work justified.

It also has the advantage that the holes in the grate are big enough for anything to fall through, so I don't have to feel bad when dropped items disappear into the bilges. How is that for total submission?

However, when done, I noticed that dropped items do not fall through the large openings directly into the bilge pump area where they might be easily retrieved. Rather, they scurried uphill to a tiny joint opening and squirmed through to imbed themselves between the two largest chunks of

ballast under the floorboards.

I simply chuckled to myself, once more finding evidence that Einstein was wrong, and maybe God really does play jokes on mere mortals.

The floor-boards in the head area took many hours of fitting and finishing to cover a mere 3 square feet of space. They are well attached to the vessel since they support the head and do not move.

A salon that is perfect for two adults, or tight for four. Grandchildren are welcome! They can sit on the berth at the end of the table and sleep on settees.

This was no minor feat, and there are about 20 components in the construction of the floorboards.

Floorboards can also keep things below them, such as ballast. If we take a knockdown, (which is likely in a monohull) the bottom of the hull is no longer the bottom of the boat, so what happens to movable ballast?

The ballast might move to the new bottom, the lee side. The boat would be less likely to return to its upright position, which could prove disastrous. It behooves us to assure that the ballast is immovable by accident.

I latched the floorboards down to the crossbeams to restrict the move-ment of the ballast. A free floorboard is under the companionway ladder over the bilge pump. It can be easily pulled up when needed, just by moving the ladder. However, when the ladder is in place it is jammed securely and cannot move.

The companionway ladder was in poor condition. It would have to be sanded, patched, and refinished. I also topped off the steps with clear, nonskid material for climbing in or out of the cabin. A brass latch on the left upper corner assures that it stays in its position under the main hatch but also locks it into the storage position in the toilet area when it is moved out from the galley.

I am surprised how well matched the varnished teak and mahogany seem. Everyone notices, and we have received more than one compliment. Perhaps they were worth all the trouble and expense. I have to admit, this came out looking pretty classy.

> *I still haven't resolved how any object dropped on the floor*
> *finds a crack to slip through and hide in the bilges,*
> *while any water that gets on the floor sits on the surface*
> *without draining into the bilges until I step on it with my warm dry socks.*

15

PORTALS AND FRESH AIR

Breathing is generally considered a good thing, but apparently Aeolus never heard of that when scheduling the winds for the month of August in the Chesapeake Bay. Not only are there no winds, but it is so hot the only thing that moves are ugly, big, blue biting flies and voracious mosquitoes.

Cheryl claims that I started whining about bugs, hatches, leaks, and ventilation as soon I saw the boat. The horrid hatches were ugly and useless and had to be replaced before I sailed. When I suggested new waterproof Plexiglas hatches with built-in bug-proof screens, I was met with "the glare" and demands that the hatches had to look right. I skulked away, but once I considered Cheryl's ideas, it struck me that we often underestimate the value of hatches on vessels. Entrances, gates, doors, and arches all attest to the value of portals in architecture; the size and appearance of them help to determine what and how a building is perceived and used. The mindsets of the users can often be influenced by the portal through which they enter.

However, on boats, hatches are chunks of plastic and screen placed anywhere they fit. Such important entities should have beauty and character to fit the designer's vision. We felt the hatches on *Rose* should look better than any other part of the boat. We discovered fanciful paintings of hatches on canal boats in England. They highlight the value of hatches to welcome and cheer all who come aboard. We tried to emulate some of the feel and whimsy in our hatches, or at least innovate freely on their designs.

This pleasant concept became a major project as we counted: a forward hatch over the V-berth; a main hatch to the companionway; a low deck hatch to the lazarette; and two cockpit-seat locker hatches. The five hatches represent 25 square feet of exterior surface, plus 25 square feet of interior surface, and all of the 50 square feet must be attractive, usable, and secure.

Hatches must provide ventilation and handle squalls, waves, wakes, mosquitoes, and crewman bashing into them. Quite a wish list, but I was the one whining, right?

It took two years to rebuild the hull and deck, and create five hatches. Fortunately, most of the work was done in *Rose*'s Dungeon, which helped the quality (since my failures could be hidden or lost). Each new or rebuilt hatch was an important part of our integrated ventilation plan as well. Too much ventilation reduces the sailing season and invites fatigue and hypothermia. Not enough ventilation burdens the crew with sleepless, sweaty nights. There is also dry rot, mildew, overheating equipment, corrosion, and vapor buildup to consider.

The original forward hatch was just nasty; it was a chunk of plywood on top of a 1 1/2-inch coaming. We sail energetically, so I eyed the low hatch suspiciously. I was confident that every time the deck was awash, the berth would get drowned. It had a center hole for a ventilator without a dorade box. I'm not small, so the 18-inch opening was the right size for me to get stuck, especially with a jacket or sweater on. It was just high enough to stumble over but too low to sit on. Our new hatch minimizes this aerobic exercise since it is high enough to sit on, low enough to step over, and strong enough to stand on. The ventilator provides a handhold, while the finish gives it an attractive traditional look.

As you look at *Rose,* your eye naturally follows the line of the bowsprit toward the cabin and intersects the forward hatch as the most important item on the foredeck. The new forward hatch is purposefully overdesigned for this role and to express our exaggerated expectations.

Intuitively, people feel that a forward-facing hatch will catch the wind and

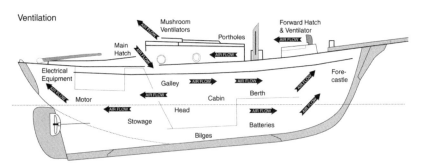

The ventilation plan is so important, we integrated this concern into our berth, motor space, head, lockers, hatches, bulkhead, and settee designs. But even more ventilation was needed.

force it through the boat, causing a forward aft flow of air that howls through the interior. It's hard to argue with this idea, since we all have experience to prove it works.

Alternatively, hatches could face aft to suck the air out of the boat. This has the advantage that they can stay open in spray or drizzle. I have noticed that experienced seaman often adopt this strategy and I am well acquainted with the type of experiences that those designs are likely based.

We were motoring through New York on a gorgeous fall day. We had the forward hatch open as we entered Hell Gate, where the East River meets Harlem River. I bore off toward the north side to avoid two tugs and a barge. As they pushed hundreds of tons of barge around the bend toward Long

Island Sound, the waters swirled into a maelstrom. It was as if the water was sucked out and we were caromed into a hole. All I could do was keep us from charging at the tugs, as the bow disappeared into a wall of green water and our prop churned in midair.

We poised at an angle for what seemed an eternity as a wall of water crashed across the deck, cabin, and into the cockpit. The open hatch was slammed back as water poured into the cabin and filled open duffel bags. That was still not enough; water sloshed through the carpeted interior into a low quarter berth as the boat righted. The boat found its footing and bounded onto smooth waters. That memorable experience confirmed my choice of having the forward hatches face aft. There was not a dry piece of carpeting, bedding, or clothing left.

It is high enough (9 inches) to stay drier and large enough (20 inches square) to fit through. Strength comes from the curve of the laminated top and ribs. The integrated hatch-dorade box design simplifies deck layout and provides an extremely rigid frame, which attaches to the deck and crossbeams with 3/8-inch bolts. Joints and areas that are susceptible to rot are sealed with epoxy.

We sanded and finished the hatch with 10 coats of varnish, then followed that with five coats of varnish without sanding. It took months, but our *piece de resistance* was ready for its public showing.

The dorade box is a sturdy base for hatch hinges and the bronze ventilator. Vents draw air from the hatch box into the dorade and ducts draw air from below the berth. Screens are built in, but netting is attached to the outside of the hatch, so it can be stowed easily, but bugs will have to work to carry it away.

Waves hit with astounding water pressure, and stories abound of leaking portholes and lost hatches! On *Rose,* a wave coming over the bow hits the bowsprit, and then the dorade box, which may induce it to flow *around* rather than *into* the hatch. A wave over the top should jam the hatch more tightly.

The ventilator is a 3-inch-diameter bronze horn, 10 inches high, with a 3x5-inch opening. The drawing power of this piece of equipment is immense if air flows freely past. The average 5- to 8-knot wind could draw 50 to 80 cubic feet of air a minute, displacing all the air in the boat (about 600 cubic feet) quickly.

Our challenge was to design pathways for that flow of air to be used. Every bulkhead, pipe, and even screen in the path of that air stream reduces flow. Since air takes the path of least resistance, it will not flow through bilges if a hatch is open.

Three rules of ventilation: We must have an inlet and an outlet. When there is no draft, hot air rises and cool air settles, and this can create a draft if a hot air outlet is higher than a cool air inlet. Air will always take the path of least resistance, so it will not flow through a small duct if a larger one is available.

The layout of *Rose* with one cabin and few barriers to airflow permits us to use lots of openings for air to move through under different weather and security situations.

The main hatch with sliding top, two solid, and one screened hatch board fits most weather/security situations. Note the rose décor and the strong wood strips across the screened area of the hatch board.

The main hatch from the bridge deck to the companionway was the simplest one to deal with. Though the mahogany boards had been badly treated, my wife was convinced they had character, so we saved them with only four or five times as much work as new ones would have taken. The topmost of the two hatch boards could be interchanged with a screened component, which was so poorly built that I built a new one.

After five coats of varnish, the scribed edges of the boards were gilded with gold paint and the rose designs were painted with great ceremony. After five more coats of varnish, we had a traditional appearance that we would not have to apologize for. We refaced the hatch edges with teak that matches the cabin edge. We also added a teak strip to the aft edge of the sliding hatch, which provides a strong edge to grab the hatch and diverts water from running back. I wish all the hatches had been as easy and produced such an attractive result.

A third main hatch board was built with louvers and screens that can be interchanged with either of the other two boards. Together these work as an extraordinarily strong screened hatch. It is reinforced so we are able to leave it in while we are visiting a harbor and still have airflow in the cabin.

Further aft, the cockpit seat hatches had their own set of challenges. They are the most heavily used part of the topsides, with people sitting, standing, and climbing on them constantly. I designed and built new hatches, along with flanges that minimize leakage into lockers and conduct water away in U-shaped channels. They are attractive like a truck because they impress with their functional power and confident feel.

The lazarette connects with the cockpit lockers, but the aft deck is 8 inches higher with lots of storage capacity. However, the small hatch was directly under the sweep of the tiller. We had to avoid jamming the tiller or breaking something to get in the locker, but we were afraid to make the hatch larger. We settled on a new hatch, though this left the original coaming (1 inch high), which is a concern. If we got pooped, a wave could lift the hatch and sweep it away, then quickly pour water into the lazarette with its electronics and controls. We opted for a pin-and-lock technique to hold the hatch with two clips and hasps. The hatch is attached to the coaming with chains so it can hang against the aft bulkhead of the cockpit when open. The hatch is light, yet strong, with plywood laminated onto curved ribs and frames. This curved surface is capped with stained 1/2-inch white cedar, so the hatch, seats, and cockpit sole match nicely, giving the aft section an integrated feeling and traditional appearance. The grooves between the cedar is caulked with black caulk, and bungee cords hold the chartbook on top of the hatch for piloting.

This great little hatch fits with no apologies. From a practical standpoint, the hatches look good, they work, some water is slowed on its way to my berth, and some bugs are deprived of blood from my body.

No matter how we try, natural ventilation may sometimes be unsatisfactory. Cheryl solved this problem with CCF (Cheryl's Cheater Fans). These seem to help us over rough spots, particularly in harbor where ventilation is restricted or blocked by larger boats. These fans work well, and since they stick to surfaces with suction cups, they are convenient anywhere onboard.

Last but not least, we still had a mildew problem when closed up for too long, so we added one of those ugly little round, solar-powered plastic vents. It leaks in heavy rain, but it does stop the mildew. We put the life ring around it so it is less noticeable.

A major concern of mine is bugs, bugs, and bugs. I hate bugs. There are pictures of my family, unbothered by bugs while sitting around in bathing suits, and me, sweating profusely in long pants and turtleneck sweaters while bugs feast on the few inches of my exposed flesh. I insist on great screens, and fortunately the portholes all had excellent screens. Overall, it seems to work well and we are pleased with the setup.

Cheryl also experimented with pillows, blankets, towels, nets, stowage stuff, and carry-on bags to maximize comfort and convenience while we retained *Rose's* traditional appearance.

If I am too cold, Cheryl is too hot, and vice versa. Because this is especially disruptive when we are sleeping onboard, Cheryl bought two large, waterproof sleeping bags that I think are very nice. They even match the interior colors nicely. When I meet God I will inquire about many curiosities in this world. One of the most confusing is why He gave men and women different thermostatic controls for their bodies and then told us to sleep together. I'll keep you posted if I get any answers.

After three years of attention to the most minute details, the hatch crusade wound to a close. Of all the projects we worked on for *Rose,* the hatches are the most obvious, rewarding, and impressive.

If you want to breathe easier and do something wonderful for your boat and yourself, make a great-looking new portal for your vessel.

16

AN INTERIOR
WORTH HAVING

When we see a classic boat, we expect the interior to be spectacular, though this may be unrealistic, since relatively few vessels are designed this way. It is nonetheless our expectation as we open the hatch and peer inside for the first time.

We feel this way about *Rose,* and it has been a challenge to live up to our expectations. *Rose* was never a luxury yacht, nor was she redesigned by us that way. She is a basic sailboat with a traditional look and finishing. She was designed to be inexpensive and stylish at the same time.

As we rebuilt her, we carefully added trim so that it seemed to have always been there. In a sense, we upgraded her while pretending to restore her to original. This yielded an exterior that appears as if it had always looked that way.

We had to start from scratch with a new interior. Though we wanted it to fit the design and intentions of the designer, we wanted it to look better than just nice. However, when everything is jammed into a space 16 feet long and 8 feet wide, it is impossible to set aside room for artistic endeavors. Attractiveness is built in, not added on to a vessel.

One concern is to keep the interior from becoming too dark with varnish and wood. We decided to use white for the inside of the cabin top and under the decks to maximize the light transmittal with Bristol beige to match the exterior on the cabinet faces. It seemed criminal to put out a lot of work making something out of high-quality wood, then covering it with paint. So, we often assumed things would be varnished and then went back and painted to taste, feeling that was easier than the converse.

The galley and toilet areas needed dry stowage before the interior could be used, so we built those cabinets early and tested them as mockups. We knew what we wanted for the salon, and with little flexibility on the amidships settees, we built those the best we could, hoping there would be few changes after the fact.

However, the last few items, cabinets and trim, were less critical, so we held off on those. Then we took her through her sea trials, shakedown cruise, and maiden voyage and kept track of our feelings and reactions and ideas. After that, we were ready to finish the interior since we had lived

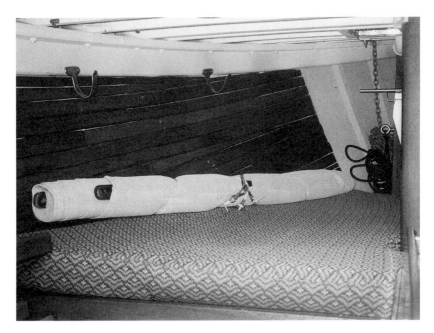

The forward part of the cabin includes a large V-berth with batteries under it. The mast goes through the center, and the sunscreen and boarding ladder hang on large bronze hooks on either side. Nonetheless, it is still large enough to be comfortable in all weather for two adults.

The focs'le is open to the cabin, with the chain and line lockers easily accessible and dry enough to avoid odor buildup. The spare Danforth anchor hangs on the bollards at the front of the berth.

under a broad range of conditions, weather, sailing, and harbors; we knew what we wanted.

The aft end of the cabin has most of the mechanical systems. We had to balance accessibility and airflow around and near such components with the need to make the interior look nice. This was especially true around the main hatch, which is the first thing one notices upon entering or leaving the cabin.

Near the hatch is the galley, the head, the auxiliary electrical system, the drive system, main power panels, and all the plumbing. We did find that stowage spaces were generally trashed, and we needed better organizing ideas.

The allied stowage areas in the aft end of the cabin were a particular mess. The small shelf across the bulkhead was always junked up, the heavy weather locker was used for everything else, and the stowage area beneath the cockpit in front of the motor was a junk pile that didn't fit elsewhere.

We added dividers and hooks to help organize things, but we are still going slowly. It will probably be a while before we have actually finished all the minor adjustments we may make in this area.

The wonderful little set of varnished shelves tucked in between the partition and the ladder exemplify my most successful efforts. It provides convenient storage for small items (horn, keys, sun block, whistle, cell phone, VHF radio, GPS, and flashlight) that must be available near the main hatch, yet does it with such style and taste that everyone remarks on it.

Toilet area stowage: lots of useful space in four dry stowage bins hold critical dry things, including paper products, towels, and miscellaneous toiletries. The countertop looks nice, but is impractical at sea.

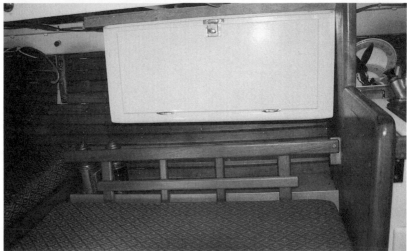

Salon cabinets have spaces for food and dry storage on the starboard side and the CD/radio, navigation charts, cruising guides, books, drawing and notepads, computer, camera, and assorted junk on the port side. Spaces below and behind the settees are perfect for small duffle bags.

Construction was tricky since it is a mere 5 inches wide and 3 feet long. Each shelf is a different height and depth for different size items, yet all can be reached from the main hatch without climbing down the ladder. Each shelf or pocket has a drain for water. It is made of interlocking pieces of 3/8-inch marine ply, glued and screwed together with six coats of varnish. It is mounted firmly, but removable to the partition that is also removable. For repairs, the ladder, shelves, and partition can be moved out of the way in

The CD player/radio has weather band and jams into space in the upper corner of the portside cabinet. Stereo speakers f ace forward from each cabinet into the berth area for great sound that stays in the cabin and does not disturb other boats in an anchorage.

less than five minutes to provide access to all the plumbing, drive, and electrical systems.

Convenience is not the only consideration. Safety is even more important since things always get broken, including people. I am particularly good at injuring myself. Years ago, I officiously gathered the kids around to show them how to shuck an oyster. I pulled one from the muddy sand of the Choptank River and fitted the point of the knife into the crack. They peered intently as I dramatically used the blade to carve a long gash in my thumb that instantly covered the oyster and my hands with blood.

The kids recoiled in disgust, unsure they wanted to eat anything that bled like that. However, as I cursed energetically, they recovered. They saw it was "only Dad" that was hurt. Once they realized that the oyster was just fine and had returned to his home in the knee-deep water, they felt much better.

It took hours to get to the hospital, but everyone survived, including the oyster. The kids (now adults with kids of their own) still remember that lesson and remind me of it, so perhaps they learned something.

However, this little lesson also points out that a first-aid kit is essential. We found a great brass case with a completely restocked Johnson & Johnson first-aid kit, which hangs in our toilet area. The kit should include serious items—even in the Chesapeake it may take hours to get to an emergency room, so some items may be lifesavers: needles and thread to stitch wounds; tourniquets to stanch blood loss; antihistamines for allergic reactions, bites, and stings; Ace bandages for splints and braces; and other medications like insulin.

I hung bronze brackets to hold the cockpit sunscreen and folding ladder against the upper edge of the ceilings along either side of the front berth. This keeps them safely out of the way, and the berth clear, so it dries more easily when it gets wet.

The teak trim across the face of the galley matches rails across the faces of the toilet-area cabinets and the salon-area cabinets.

Last but not least, the teak trim along the edges of the two partial bulkheads dividing the settee/salon area from the toilet and galley areas made a tremendous difference in the appearance and properly finished interior. The teak is nicely rounded and 2 inches square with a 3/4-inch-deep groove that fits over the edge of the 1/2-inch plywood bulkhead. Properly fitted, they strengthen and stabilize the bullhead edges, even against the force of a human body thrown around by wakes from a large vessel or offensive powerboats.

A lot of such wood-crafting are attempts to cover up cracks, holes, nicks, and dents created in the process of assembling the structure. It may be as little as an undulation caused by a slight wobble while sanding, or a slight crack from a misfit joint, or as ugly as a 1/4-inch hole a 1/4 inch deep with a screwhead in it. No matter, each item must be carefully filled or plugged, sanded, finished and painted or varnished.

The two amidships cabinets mount almost flush to the underside of the deck, basically hanging from the deck beams on either side of the cabin. They are designed to deflect dripping water from any source away from their contents and each pocket has drains to help keep dry items stowed in the cabinets. The portside cabinet includes a large pocket for navigation charts, books, and instruments, as well as room for a small stereo. There is also a large space for books, dry stowage, and cameras.

The stereo system is built into the two salon cabinets with the speakers directed forward into the berth area. Despite the small interior, this permits the sound to permeate the salon with a richness we did not expect, yet it cannot be heard outside the boat at all.

The starboard-side cabinet has a closing front door that opens downward and provides about 3 cubic feet of dry stowage, mostly for paper goods and foodstuffs. It also includes two pockets for small items. The forward section of each cabinet has a speaker from the CD/radio system and a small shelf and hooks for personal items accessible from the berth but almost invisible in the rest of the cabin.

As the interior took on its final shape and appearance, many little items made all the difference to the finished vessel.

The radio antenna was a bit of a challenge, since we were seeking traditional appearance and the fewest possible holes in the boat. I installed the antenna inside the cabin and attached it to the inside wall, almost invisibly sticking up next to the corner lamp. It is hardly noticeable, and it seems to have good reception even though it is only 3 feet above the waterline. The whole installation is quite nice—a merger of practicality and beauty.

The inclusion of the CD player, a rose vase, and other small amenities changed the interior toward the more comfortable side, but one artistic touch made a major difference in the overall look, especially at first glance. We also want the folding boarding ladder and cockpit sunscreen stored safely and attractively, so we made four bronze hooks (we removed the chrome from life-ring hooks to expose bronze). The hooks mount on either side of the berth at the top edge of the ceilings just below the deck, with the sunscreen rolled up on the port side and the folded ladder hanging on the starboard side. The partition between the companionway and the toilet area incorporates two painted panels borrowed from our canal boat inspirations. Cheryl painted a scene with a castle, a lake, and a boat, and a tall panel of roses with brightly painted borders, adding a touch of lightness and a wonderful conversation piece to the main hatch.

We still needed curtains, covers, storage pockets, and a sun cover. I was up to my ears in work, so I insisted that Cheryl handle the sewing. She agreed and borrowed a sewing machine from our daughter-in-law. She also bought a rose-patterned shower curtain for the divider curtains that pick up many of the colors in the cabin and the cushions. However, she eventually claimed that she could not do as good a job as I did on the boat and so gave me her permission to do the sewing.

Cheryl also collects heavy-weather gear, pets' life preservers, grandkids' life preservers, adult life preservers, and our inflatable life preservers. Her soft touch extends to clothing and stowage bags, nets, windbreakers, *Rose* caps, and more.

These last few steps to truly finish the boat were extremely time-consuming. Every little step seemed to take forever, and months slipped by as we slowly approached the end. We changed our minds and redid things on occasion, but we can proudly claim that the interior looks pretty good. The colors balance well, and the interior is neither too dark nor lacking brightness.

We do not have to apologize for it, as long as you are happy looking at a sailing boat, not a classic yacht.

> *With bright work and Cheryl's canal boat paintings on the partition, we declared* Rose *complete, a mere six years after we found her.*

Cheryl saved this abandoned wood sailboat from a date with a bonfire. It became Rose and is the basis for this story.

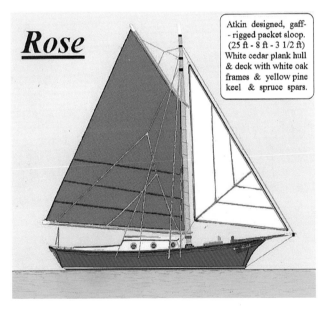

Rose

Atkin designed, gaff-
- rigged packet sloop.
(25 ft - 8 ft - 3 1/2 ft)
White cedar plank hull
& deck with white oak
frames & yellow pine
keel & spruce spars.

My idea of Cheryl's dreamboat, drawn before the boat even arrived in our backyard. The drawing became our guide, and the dream did become a reality— although it took more time, work, and money than we ever imagined.

Hull refastening forced us to focus our initial paint and bottom-coating stripping efforts on the areas of the ribs and end-joint blocks. Once the hull planks were firmly attached to the ribs and keel, we completed the rest of the stripping.

The first hull plank that popped loose and started the refastening project. Note that the joint is between ribs at a block of wood that was later replaced. Most of the planks were loose by the time we started refastening.

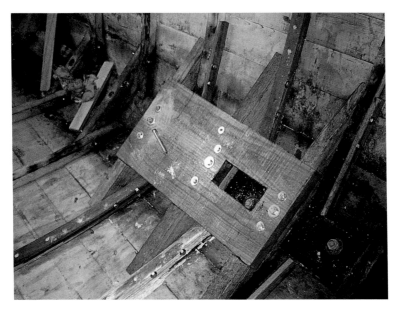

New ribs, mast step, and crossbeams are perfect inside the refastened hull as we prepare for the new interior. Sanding and grinding, followed by sealer and a fungicide-based paint, sealed the hull before new ceilings were installed.

The stripping, patching, sanding, and filling that were necessary to get a fair surface were easy compared to the refastening.

The transom/stern rail is a massive work of art that ties together the aft deck, transom, and the sheer line toe-rails into a pleasing and useful form. Without professional help we would have never achieved these excellent results.

We collected and played with hundreds of rose drawings, designs, and ideas, but everything was too difficult, too big, too bright, too dull, or too complex.

English canal boat decorations with lots of flowers inspired simple painted roses for our nameplates and hatches, as well as Rose's companionway panel. Utility shelves in the space next to the ladder hold GPS and VHF units, a light, and other small items.

Once we were into the fray, we decided that the main hatch boards had to have roses, too. With this addition, we passed outlandish and went straight for outrageous. Nameplates were a big project and their design took a long time. The solution was simpler than we imagined, though it took a lot of work. Cheryl painted the roses with oil paints and covered them with several coats of varnish.

The transom features a removable sign that has a compound curve with thick, bronze letters and roses painted around and in the letters. It is centered between the stern light and the pump drains.

The bow nameplate has recessed letters and painted roses with a hinged joint to fit the shape of the hull and bow area. It is attached solidly to handle bad weather, and it is protected from docks by the side chains on the bowsprit.

The finished bow looks great with the bowsprit, nameplates, and large hatch framed by black chains and topped with a small teak safety platform and an anchor. With its heavy ground tackle, it is also extremely functional and has weathered several brutal storms and some serious sailing.

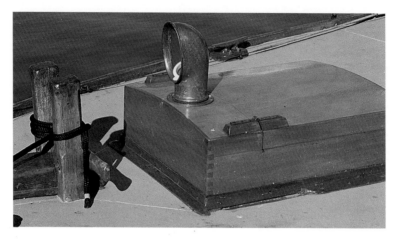

The forward hatch is the foredeck's piece de resistance. It is attractive, solid, and it incorporates a large vent and dorade box and a seat for hauling lines. The vent can be rotated for different weather and sailing situations. The small area ahead of the hatch box is convenient line stowage. After months of work, the topsides came together beautifully. Unfortunately, the plank decks leaked terribly and were eventually covered with cork.

Cleating blocks with winches and cleats. The large tapered blocks lock into the cockpit coaming and cover old engine vent holes. Two-inch bronze winches and cleats were found at a boat flea market. I manufactured a bronze handle for the winches.

The main hatch has vented and screened hatch boards, properly decorated with rose emblems, while teak trim gives the cockpit a finished look. The Atkin-design cockpit, bridge deck, cabin top, and decks are laid out to provide large, easy-to-use sail- and line-handling areas that seem appropriate for a much larger boat. However, with all the space, we find that we have a tendency to clutter the decks with too much stuff.

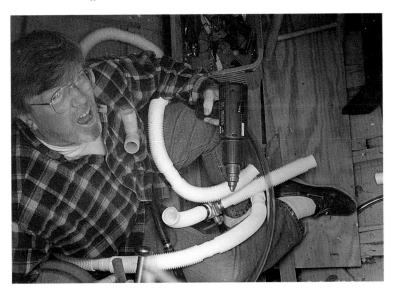

#%!#@&#! Plumbing and I do not play well together.

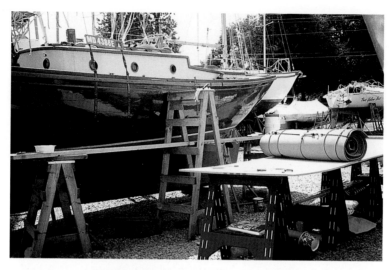

Eventually, we gave up on sealing the plank decks and decided to cover them with 1/4-inch cork sheets. Scaffolds surrounded the boat and a 4x16-foot setup table was used to lay out, cut, and fit the cork, which we glued to the deck with 5200 caulk.

It took several days to cure the adhesive and lots of weight to flatten the cork. Because the caulk was thick, some places took weeks to fully cure. The cork aged to a gray color, so the next season we sanded the decks and sealed them with caramel-colored sealer. They look great and are holding up very well.

Copper sheathing wrapped around the keel and attached with copper nails and 5200 caulking has protected the keel from groundings, which occur frequently in the shallow Chesapeake Bay.

The finished front deck was complete with new king planks and restored bollards, trimmed with black polysulfide caulking and caramel-colored linseed oil stain. The leading edge was sealed with copper plate and caulking before the refinished bowsprit and hardware was installed. The deck was later covered with cork.

The bowsprit is a spar and a key part of the standing rigging. Held in place by the chains, it braces against the two teak bollards, which go down to the keel through the deck. The anchor rides on the port side with room for another anchor on the starboard side and a platform between. Note the capstan and hawsholes to the chain locker in the focs'l.

The bowsprit resists the upward and sideways pull of the jib forestay and mast and is tuned with the forestay, sail stay, and chains below and on each side. The chains are attached to the hull with bronze chainplates bolted through the keel or ribs. Tension can bend the bowsprit several inches during sailing.

Halyards lead to the foot of the mast and tie off to a teak crossbeam with a small winch at a convenient height. It looks like a bit of a mess, but it works better than it looks. It is also much quieter than modern rigs with harder ropes and hollow aluminum masts.

The mast boot is heavy canvas with clamps around the mast and deck collar. It slows water on its trek to my berth, while allowing the mast and deck to move as designed. The line is from the dock bumpers, stowed between the mast and the leading edge of the cabin. (Right) Tapered wood wedges are driven between the mast/deck collar (6-inch reinforced plastic composite sewer pipe flange) and the mast to hold the mast in place.

Not only do they look cool, but mast hoops are also strong. Some people even climb the mast on them.

The masthead seems confusing but is not bad once you sort out the booms, lines, blocks, and shrouds. Rose's mast is shorter than modern ones, so it is easier to go aloft to fix problems.

The yoke (center left) allows the boom to move and stay correctly aligned for the sails and lines. The yoke handles tremendous stress and is made from strong white oak, with bronze through-bolts and leather padding on the surfaces that make contact with the mast.

Nine bronze chainplates are attached with silicon bronze bolts through the hull and into oak braces.

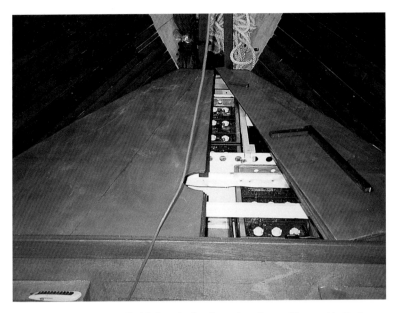

Three battery boxes installed below the berth retain a dozen 65-pound batteries, even in heavy seas, while providing room for airflow and wiring. The 780 pounds of batteries also function as ballast.

The mast sets through the middle of the berth but is not very intrusive because the berth is 7 feet wide. A sun cover and boarding ladder mount out of the way to hooks on either side. The table is usually stowed at night to free up the open space in the middle of the cabin.

Berth and settee cushions are made from a heavy-duty material with a rose-colored fleur de lis pattern over thick closed-cell foam. The backs are made of a heavy net material to allow airflow. The berth cushions taper from 2 feet wide in the bow to about 7 feet wide amidships. The settee cushions are sized for grandchildren to sleep on or for us to comfortably lounge on while reading.

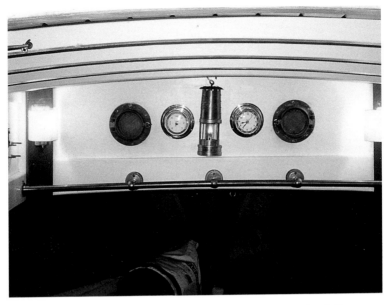

The view of the forward cabin bulkhead as one enters from the main hatch. Two portholes framed by lights in each corner leave room for a clock and barometer. Over the salon table there is a nice spot for an oil lamp, along with a solar electric vent. The brass bar is great for getting in and out of the berth or as a grab bar in a seaway.

The folding salon table is the center of the cabin and salon area. The table can be easily moved out of the way. It was also my first attempt at building furniture and is my pride and joy in the interior.

When both leaves are folded down, the table is easy to move around. When closed, it offers a convenient 4-inch-wide surface with a 2-inch lip for some storage and a handhold. Each side folds open separately.

The compact galley squeezes a sink with two water supplies, a gimballed stove, and trash compartment across the front. Dish and implement stowage is behind, with food stowage beneath and in the ice chest under the ladder.

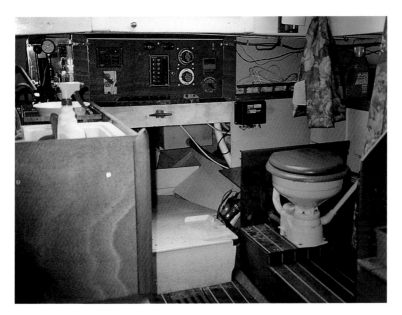

This view aft with the companionway ladder and toilet partition removed shows stowage areas in the rear. The ladder, small shelves, and toilet-area partition are movable and provide a great deal of privacy and the ease of repair and maintenance.

A view of the cabin's aft section shows the galley, power panel, ice chest, ladder, shelves, and toilet area. The galley has a large, well-insulated ice chest accessible with the ladder in place. It can be moved to gain access to the aft stowage compartment. The curtains partition the area, the Sun Shower hangs in the hatch, and the ladder stows in the toilet area for more space in the galley.

The stove, during its final rebuild and conversion from pressurized kerosene to propane. I bought two propane camping stoves, cannibalized the burners, and repiped them to fit inside. I saved the original parts in case someone ever wants to restore it. The stove has two burners, an oven, and a grill. It looks great and provides plenty of ballast for the boat. It didn't work very well until we converted it to propane.

A brass first-aid kit hanging over the toilet is loaded with more serious contents than Band-Aids, aspirin, and suntan lotion. It was a great find at a flea market, and it still contained all of its original supplies, which we replaced.

Rose's original 40-year-old gas engine. Anybody need a very heavy, but generally functional 12-horsepower Universal Motors (UM2) engine with rotted exhaust, questionable instruments, and a long gear control lever that belongs to a tractor or some other motorized mechanism?

We bought a used Yamaha golf cart with new batteries, cables, and a complete checkup. We cannibalized the motor, controls, and power system to build Rose's first electric drive system. Unfortunately, it failed, and we replaced it.

My friend Jack's sympathetic expressions helped us through the motor crisis. However, his windup key idea did get more than casual discussion after the problems, delays, expenses, failures, and embarrassments we had with the electric drive system.

The power control center (left) for all three electric systems is under the bridge deck and main hatch. It can be reached through the companionway ladder, between the galley and toilet area, and over the main ice chest.

The instrument panel on the cockpit's forward bulkhead (accessible from the cabin through the bulkhead) includes a compass, depth sounder, knotmeter, and auxiliary power backed to the electrical panel in the cabin.

The drive control panel on the cockpit's aft bulkhead mates to the controller in the lazarette and features a forward-aft lever, fast-slow lever, key switch, reverse sounder, and forward-reverse light indicators. On other vessels the Rose cap might be optional.

The heavy weather locker (with the red coats) in the toilet area is designed to let air circulate and provide easy access to the stowage around it. It is usually a junk hole for dirty laundry, but during a few days of rainy or stormy weather, it becomes essential for sanity in the small interior.

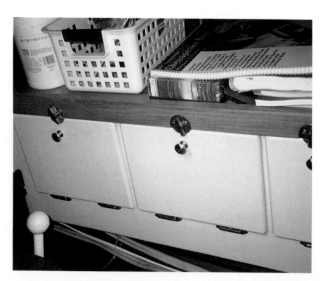

Toilet area lockers and counters are crucial for stowage, and they incorporate a lot of useful space in a small area. The four different-sized bins match the ceilings behind and boast large surfaces. We may add more cabinets in place of the attractive but inconvenient countertop. All interior cabinets are painted Bristol beige and offset with teak and holly. The ceilings are varnished mahogany and the cabin top and walls are painted bright white.

Salon cabinets behind the settees have space for dry food stowage, navigation charts, books, a radio/CD player and speakers, a camera, and other items. Space below is used for small duffel bags. The cabinets were built with marine plywood and teak, and they were designed to direct water away from their contents. They work well, but we have to avoid carrying too much junk because they have limited capacities.

Rose, ready to be launched, and astride a hydraulic trailer for a short trip to the massive lift for her real "splashing." She was lowered into the water and retrieved three times prior to prepare for the real thing. We pulled her several times later as well.

Cheryl is quite happy with her boat after four years of work at home and two more down in northeast Maryland. The boat is small but seems big, and she is perfect for day sailing and weekending. Here, Cheryl demonstrates the style for which Rose is famous—looking good!

Rose took a while to find her footing, but she loves to sail, particularly off-wind. Here she dampens the rail with a bit of spray as she takes a sea in a nice blow. We have never buried the rail, despite several attempts both in fun and stupidity.

New sails look good and help performance more than expected. Rose plows into a nice wind at a cruising speed of around 4 1/2 knots. The main is partially reefed in this photo but still retains a usable shape. Note how low the gaff boom is on the mast.

The gaff rig looks spectacular on a good reach as Rose approaches hull speed and digs in for a serious sail. Note how straight she stands when going correctly. Six thousand pounds of displacement and a low aspect rig do make a difference. Most 25-footers would heel twice as far in this fairly heavy wind.

After sailing, this is what it's all about. Queenstown on the Chester River is like many spots on the Chesapeake Bay. One of our favorite gunkholes is only a few hours from civilization, but it offers a lovely anchorage with few visitors, great sunsets, swans, fishing, crabbing, and oysters.

A good boarding ladder with safety lines and comfortable floating cushions is necessary for great gunkholing. Note how the ladder hooks over the toe-rail, snaps into notches on the bumper rail, and fits the curve of the hull. It folds down flat and stows easily over the berth.

Our Walker Bay 8 dinghy, Thorn, is used by Cheryl, grandchildren, and dogs when gunkholing. Unfortunately, it is too big for the deck and must be towed when needed.

Looking cool, calm, and sophisticated is the key to gunkholing. Our granddaughter Alanna was only a few months old in this photo, but a life jacket and ring worked fine. We plan for her to win the America's Cup, but we'll wait until she talks to discuss it with her.

17

BACK TO SEA

In 1997, we moved *Rose* to our backyard for repairs. The repairs multiplied and her visit dragged into years. Slowly, she took on the mantle of a rebuilt boat nestled in the lush green hills of Chester County. *Rose* formed many friendships over those years. Neighbors stopped by to see how she was; they stroked her sides and trim to affirm that she was getting better. They empathized with her, asking about her operations and developments.

She was a fixture as children grew up and new neighbors turned their new houses into homes. *Rose* was accustomed to the country, her yard, and her adoptive home where she hid amongst trees and shrubs. Four years later, it was time to look to *Rose*'s future. We had worked on her enough; now she could not be finished until she was in the water.

She could not be outfitted until the interior was installed, and she could not be rigged until the mast was stepped. The interior, ballast, and batteries could not be installed until she was floating properly.

It was just a day in March when the time came to send her back to the sea. We had several weeks of work to do to get her ready for her move, so I planned to arrange it in the next month or so. It shouldn't have been hard, but nobody knew how hard she would fight to stay in Chester County.

0800: First cup of coffee in hand, I called the marina owner. He said he could fit us in, but we had to get there soon. They would be too busy in a few weeks to caulk and paint. After that, they wouldn't be able to do it until July, a three-month delay. I wanted to go sailing sooner, but I was unaware of *Rose*'s objections.

0815: I called the hauler. He said, "I'm busy. How's May?" I explained that the marina would be busy, and our yard was low so it would be swamp by then. He responded, "Well, how's today?"

I offhandedly responded in my half-awake condition, "Let me check. I'll call back."

0820: I walked outside and tested the ground. The temperature was 28 degrees and the ground was frozen. I was inspired that a load of gravel spread along the path would assure traction.

0825: I checked the weather. The temperature was expected to reach 35 degrees, and it was supposed to be dry this morning. Yet, a warm front was moving in.

0830: The boat was wrapped in winter covers. I called my son, "Can you give me a hand?"

"Yes."

0835: Masts were not ready to ship. I called a friend. "Can you postpone your jobs and give me a hand?"

"Yes."

0840: The boat was not ready for transport. I called the gravel supplier. "Can you get a truckload of gravel over here right away?"

"Yes."

0845: I called the marina. "Can you take us today?"

"Yes."

"Can you put her in the water, caulk, and paint soon?"

"Yes."

"Can you stay late, if we move now?"

"Yes."

0855: *Rose* was hiding under winter covers, protected by scaffolds and incomplete projects. However, apparently having heard too many yeses in a row, I was fully delusional. I called the hauler and said, "Yes!"

After four years of country living, Rose looks almost ready to go back to the sea, but she fought to stay in comfortable Chester County, making that day one of the worst days in my life, and maybe Rose's life too.

He responded, "OK, I'll see you in two hours." I don't know whether my biorhythms were off, or if it was the phase of the moon, but one of the worst days of my life had just begun, and my first cup of coffee was cold.

0900: My son showed up. We had no time to dismantle the fence, so we took wire-cutters to the wire and sawed the posts.

0910: Before the fence was down, the gravel truck arrived. But he slowed too much as he backed in and the heavy truck broke through the frozen surface with tons of gravel. Unable to go forward or backward, he dumped the load 40 feet from where we needed it without spreading it. He was still stuck.

0930: Painstakingly, we dug the truck out by hand and filled the holes he created. It took an hour to get free, but my semifrozen gravel path was just a pipe dream. *Rose* smugly eyed the huge mess of holes, frozen mud, and gravel.

1030: Frantic, we spread gravel by hand while Cheryl rushed to get wire fencing to reinforce the path and help support the surface.

1100: Sweating in the cold morning air, abusing muscles I didn't know I had, we appraised the status and knew it couldn't be done. My third cup of coffee was cold.

1105: Frank the hauler showed up. A crusty master sergeant, he didn't listen to our pain and suffering. He drove two hours to do a job, and he would do it. As we dug in again, I sensed *Rose* glaring at us.

1110: Cheryl returned with wire fencing for the path to report a forecast calling for one of the wettest springs in history, "So do it now, or else!"

1115: We dug in to move tons of rock on top of two layers of wire fencing to stabilize the mess. *Rose* balefully watched our erratic progress.

1200: Frank was impatient, so he backed his 60-foot rig assertively down our pitiful path. As he turned toward *Rose,* the trailer slid into a hole from the gravel truck and jackknifed. He pulled forward and got stuck.

1215: Unable to free him with digging, gravel, and boards, we hooked another four-wheel-drive to the rig and with both trucks, barely extricated the rig from the melting mass of earth, gravel, and fencing.

1230: Frantic gravel moving improved the surface as our pain and exhaustion grew. My fifth cup of cold coffee was discarded and clouds moved in as the predicted warm front materialized overhead.

1255: Impatient with my whining, Frank tried again. With incredible brazenness, he blasted backward at full speed in four-wheel drive and did a 12-wheel slide as he careened toward *Rose.* Impressively, he missed a tree

Master Sergeant (Ret.) Frank Pinder arrived with an impressive hydraulic trailer and a lot of rain in tow. With a "Damn the mud! Full speed astern!" he whipped toward the pad to drag Rose from her home

with inches to spare and stopped under the bowsprit with no damage other than a few more holes in the yard.

1300: Our cheers died as the clouds opened and poured forth a steady drizzle on our works. Wretched, we split our efforts between a makeshift road and preparing an uncooperative *Rose* for transport.

1330: *Rose*'s warm winter covers were cruelly stripped, and equipment was ripped from her embrace and thrown into a pile. The rig sank deeper into the backyard each time we juggled it to lift the wet, naked vessel.

1345: Drizzle begat rain as the yard morphed into a dismal swamp. Frank the hauler said it was time to go or he would never get out. *Rose* groaned as she was lifted bodily off her stands by cold hydraulic arms.

1355: The diesel cranked up to a roar and the rig, loaded with a 6,000-pound boat, accelerated down a slight grade. Wheels spinning and mud flying, Frank deftly whipped around the curve and toward the road. But *Rose* would not yield. He slowed even as the diesel roared and wheels spun. Halfway to the road, he cut power and the rig settled into the mire.

1405: We tried to pull the 70-foot rig out with both four-wheel-drive trucks working and every weapon in our arsenal. Nonetheless, *Rose* settled deeper into the rich humus of the Brandywine Valley.

1410: We briefly debate the possibility that more rain might float the boat off the trailer, and then we could sail her across the field and down the Brandywine. We yielded and called the towing company. My sixth cup was mostly rainwater.

1420: The tow truck arrived, looked at the scope of our disaster and the 10 tons of rig and vessel sinking into the yard, and disappeared. The rain became a downpour and axles sank into muck. I found coffee and a dry spot.

1430: A bigger tow truck showed up, admitting they only came back since we knew them and had done business together. A winch from the road and 100 feet of heavy steel cable slowly dragged the rig from its muddy entrapment. *Rose* seemed to fight each movement.

Sometimes it's better not to know, like when someone picks up four years of hard work and money, and drives off with it. The powerful truck and hydraulic-armed trailer were impressive, though scary.

1500: Freed from the morass, Frank headed south with *Rose,* and I followed. I called to ask the marina crew to wait. A groan of acceptance on the other end indicated they had had a great day too.

1730: The yard crew and Frank unloaded *Rose* onto jacks so they could leave for homes and dinners. In the darkening misty chill, it occurred to me that strangers were handling *Rose* for the first time. I gave her a reassuring pat before leaving her amongst the plastic-wrapped cocoons in the boatyard.

She was yanked from home and dragged to a strange place with no warning. Everyone was in an evil humor in a freezing downpour. She looked bedrag-

Days after Rose departed for the sea, we found this perfectly styled wind vane that sits on our roof as a memento.

gled and out of place in the rain-swept scene, lines dangling awkwardly, toe-rails broken, and new scratches from the experience. She looked lost and disoriented, reminding me of how the kids looked as they headed off to college or to the navy. As a parent, you know that leaving is the right thing, and you are excited for them, but there is a sweet sadness with the change and concern about the future.

1815: I drank the cold eighth cup of coffee as I drove home. It tasted terrible, but I needed it. The worst day of my life was drawing to a close.

The next day I fixed the fence for the dogs, and *Rose*'s absence made the rainy scene more dismal. That week, everyone noticed that *Rose* was gone. Neighbors and friends stopped and asked what had happened to her. Years later, people still identify our house as "the place where *Rose* lived."

> *There was an odd happening shortly after* Rose *left.*
> *I found a wind vane that was an image of a rose,*
> *which Cheryl insisted we buy.*

> *We chuckled that* Rose *was only gone a few days*
> *when she returned in this small analogue.*
> *Cheryl's reaction was that it was only right,*
> *and that there was nothing strange about it.*

18

DRY BILGES:
A JOKE FOR WOOD BOATS

I've heard the phrase "dry bilges," but I have never in 50 years of boating seen a dry bilge. Even if the boat were not leaking somewhere, condensation would leave evidence. No matter what kind of boat or how well it is constructed, water collects in the bilges.

The first task is to minimize the water collection rate. Not only did we seal the hull the best way possible, but we also sealed the deck and created drains off the deck and out of the cockpit. We redesigned the hatches to reject any attempt by water to get inside. We designed and built a new mast deck collar and put a new canvas boot around the mast. We carefully surveyed vents and portholes, and we did what we could to assure that water would not enter. I even added teak trim across the lid of the main hatch to divert water to the sides.

Preparing the hull to go back in the water, Todd Brinkman, painter and artist supreme, did the paint and boot strip professionally to bring her up to snuff.

Of course, water will come in through the hull. We had already refastened it properly to get planks to match up with each other so it would be strong and waterproof. However, with a wood boat, it is water that makes the hull waterproof, by swelling the planks so that the wood presses hard against the next plank.

The wood hull was treated as if it were almost new, even though we had rebuilt it using original wood where possible. It had been out of the water at least six years, making the wood dry and shrunken. The saga of *Rose's* next few months is complicated and the process of sealing a wooden hull is an art form in itself. It took weeks to prepare, but in April, we began.

On April 15, they carried her to the crane and sling and placed a large pump on board. The first job was to suspend it in the water until the wood swelled up with a good moisture content. Lots of silt entered our pristine interior, so we installed nothing until the hull was sealed.

By May 3, the wood had swollen to what it should be so Don Green and the Bay Boat Works people put her ashore to wash out the mud and silt.

They also put cotton into her joints and caulked them without getting too aggressive.

A little more drying, a coat of bottom paint, and *Rose* was back in the water. Once she adjusted to the wet environment and could float on her own, we loaded the weight on board that she would normally carry, and then added three 50-gallon drums of water to simulate the weight of people and consumables.

The bilge is no deeper than 12 inches, and in some places only 3 inches below the floorboards. Drainage through the bilges is restricted by ribs and crossbeams with holes drilled in them. Since these are small to avoid weakening the crossbeams, they tend to easily plug with dirt.

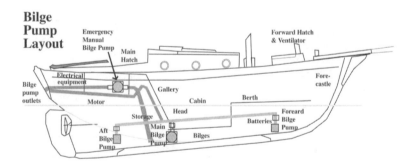

A good hull and decks, ventilation, and bilge pumps are just part of getting and keeping dry bilges. How many bilge pumps? How big? Power demands, location, piping, and valves complicate issues.

Our bilge holds movable ballast for stability. This is odd stuff, essentially 800 pounds of lead in the form of ingots from 2 to 50 pounds. These ingots are as small as 3 inches in diameter and an inch thick, and up to 1 foot square and 3 inches thick. The ingots taper about 20 degrees, so even jammed together, water slips around them. We trimmed the boat with the movable ballast until she floated exactly on the waterline.

After a week of adjustment and final ballast trim, we pulled her again. We cleaned, sanded, and painted the hull and the bottom. We installed the motor and batteries permanently with a temporary electrical system to do commissioning and outfitting. The interior was washed out again, plugs were screwed into place, the through-hull fittings were closed, and bilge pumps were installed.

I have not been too picky about bilge pumps in the past. However, the standard for *Rose* was higher than that. Since the vessel is driven by wind or electricity, we don't want the bilge pumps to use much electricity. It is important that they do the minimum possible pumping and that they operate in an efficient manner. Pumps that are too small run a lot, but pumps that are too large use a lot of power when they run.

I tested the pumps using a 50-gallon drum to assure that they would work when we installed them and measured the power draw at the height we expected to pump the water. Incredibly, the specifications were often wrong or misleading. Unfortunately, I did not think to measure one crucial feature: the size of objects the pump would pass without locking up.

Copper sheathing was bent and wrapped around the keel with copper nails and caulking to protect the keel in groundings and minimize bugs eating it.

The literature encouraged smaller pumps, but the larger ones were more efficient and effective. Several were better in every way I could measure. A bilge pump four sizes larger (2,000 gallons per hour) than the manufacturer suggests (500 gallons per hour) in a 25-foot boat worked properly.

On May 10 we set *Rose* in the water and loaded on the weight she would normally carry, including spars, batteries, and motor. We moved ballast until she trimmed perfectly on the waterline. On May 23, after a week of adjustments, we pulled her again and cleaned her; Todd Brinkman sanded and painted the hull, bottom, and boot strip. We also installed the motor, ballast, batteries, bulkheads, settees, and flooring frames, as well as a temporary electrical system so we could commission properly. On June 10, we had a rigger come in to set up the standing and running rigging since we had never done it before.

I mounted the masthead light I had built with a solar cell to run all night with no wire to the batteries. We ran rigging and slipped the hoops and mast boot onto the mast. The interior was washed, plugs screwed in, through-hull fittings closed, and bilge pumps tested with the final wash out.

She was ready to go back in permanently, except for one detail. We installed copper plates on the keel, so when we run aground there will be protection from nasties like worms and such.

On June 23, after many trials, we finally launched the boat. Though this was launching for commissioning, we broke out a bottle and did the deed with the Bay Boat Works crew.

After 51 months of work, Rose is launched by an overhead lift at Bay Boat Works in June 2001.

Incredibly, she was tight and secure enough that we didn't need the big pump the yard had in her. After a few minutes, our own bilge pumps were doing the trick.

They cycled frequently for a few days, but soon they handled the flow by coming on every 10 minutes and pumping for seconds. This rate slowly improved but seems to be typical of what we should expect. Based on the care with which we rebuilt the hull, and got her ready to go in the water, it comes as no surprise that she leaks very little.

By the second year, it was down to once every 15 minutes, but we did keep her in the water through the winter. When we go out and sail particularly hard, and have a lot of rain and spray, the rate seems to go up, so the collection and leakage rate is a variable.

During commissioning she was pulled two more times as we fought our way through a host of problems. It took months to complete her outfitting, but Rose was launched for sea trials at Bay Boat Works in July 2001.

I'm amazed how many issues I have dealt with regarding dry bilges. Given the opportunity to complicate things, I always rise to the occasion, so on *Rose,* we have not one, not two, not even three, but *four* bilge pumps.

The main pump is aft at the galley, and handles the bilges most of the time. It is larger and permanently wired to the battery system with a level switch. It also drains the shower area and water that runs down the ladder from the main hatch.

Two small electric pumps fore and aft drain any water trapped that cannot easily get to the main pump. They could also help out the main pump in the case of an emergency. Both of these work off a switch and an automatic level switch.

These three feed into the drain line through one-way valves so that water will not flow backward and exhaust a drain in the transom.

I added one-way valves to the lines to minimize backflow, which causes unnecessary pumping. I also set the drain lines so that they run down toward the stern once the pumps hoist the water above a neutral point and prevent wash back from the exhaust outlet. A large manual emergency pump in the cockpit operates independent of the other three. It mounts in the portside cockpit locker and drains through a transom fitting.

On the transom, two vents for the sewage and water tanks are at the top on either side of the custom light. They connect via 6-foot plastic tubing to the highest point on the tanks. The two drains down below the nameplate are for bilge pumps. The one on the right (starboard) is a single outlet from the three electric bilge pumps that are connected to the single outlet with reverse-flow valves to prevent the water pumped out from returning back to the bilges. The drain on the left (port) is a larger drain from the manual emergency pump located in the portside cockpit locker.

Stepping the mast was not hard with a crane and three knowledgeable people. All rigging, lines, hoops, and boot were on the mast as we lowered and set it in place through the deck fitting onto the mast step.

The bilge drainage systems interconnect through lines and one-way valves to a transom drain. There are seven different sized hoses and fittings in the bilge pump network.

I naively expected stuff I bought to operate the way they were advertised. This led to lots of disappointment and aggravation. It took a total of seven bilge pumps to finally get three that worked properly, and I rebuilt the hand bilge pump as well.

I strongly recommend that anyone doing this job test the device before you waste time installing it. Especially test the claim that the bilge pump will pump objects of such and such a size; most pumps we tried failed on objects far smaller than they claimed were passable. In addition, we found the automatic floats jammed on almost anything.

One stated it would handle objects up to a 1/2 inch in diameter, and then it fouled on sawdust trapped in the bilge. I found pumps jammed on splinters of wood, small nuts and washers, sawdust, and 1/4-inch-long electric wire casings. All of this is small debris that cannot be avoided in the bilge of a restored boat.

In addition to the hodge-podge of ill-fitting parts, there are quality issues too—I bought nine one-way check valves but could use only five.

A manual emergency pump in the cockpit scavenges water from the bilge out a transom fitting. We discovered the valves were installed backward at the factory. This required a rebuild of a new pump and could have been disastrous if we had not tested it before our shakedown cruise.

Bilges are a good example of a serious challenge. Wood feeds fungus, especially mildew and dry rot, and constant moisture with wood provides the perfect environment for these fungi to grow and wreak their havoc. Wood boats often have openings high on the hull sides for air to get out of the bilges and into the cabin, flowing between the hull and the ceilings, but how does it get in?

We replaced the floorboards in *Rose* and added a small grate under the companionway ladder to let air into the bilge area. We left small spaces at the top of each crossbeam and the floorboard lying on a crossbeam, so air gets to sections isolated by crossbeams. This should help keep us dryer, while minimizing fungus and odors.

I'd just like the bilge water to go away.

People were surprised that Rose *trimmed exactly to the waterline, but the line was based on the design drawing and we weighed everything as we built it to keep her at design weight. When we put her in the water, we used movable ballast to trim her port-starboard and forward-aft until she sat on the line as her design specified.*

19

SILENCE OF THE SEA, PART II:
GOLF CARTS SHOULD
STAY ON DRY LAND

In our original plan, an electric golf cart motor (not an engine) with a custom flange replaced *Rose's* gas engine. However, nothing could be installed and tested in the real environment until after the boat was put back into the water and thoroughly sealed up. As soon as the bilges were dry and the boat was trimmed, we installed bulkheads, battery trays, and batteries under the berth. Then we were ready to install the motor below the cockpit and the controls in the cockpit and lazarette. We had tested the system and labeled every connection before we packed it up to take it down to the marina. In our minds we were already out in the bay, set to go sailing as we made battery, charger, controller, and motor connections, and then cajoled the coupling onto the prop shaft.

After a few hours of battery charging, we were ready. We checked charge level, confirmed voltages at junctions, and searched for shorts. The anticipation was so strong, we could taste it. I turned the key and the fuses blew instantly.

Two days and a dozen fuses later, we had fixed an erroneously connected wire and a few other problems. We thought we were ready to go again. However, the system failed in seconds. We continued our diagnosis and repairs over the next week, pulled the motor out twice, and yanked the control panel three times before we felt it was right. We turned it on and it ran for a dozen seconds to our cheers, then died ignominiously.

More testing and repairs yielded forward power by the end of the next week. Buoyed by even a grudging victory, we tried reverse, but the coupling unscrewed under stress and the motor spun furiously, while the prop sat placidly in the water. Now we had a mechanical failure. Nothing else could possibly go wrong, could it?

With mixed emotions, we pulled the motor and machined the coupling again as we slipped into week three. After reinstalling and rewiring a rat's nest of wiring with our changes, we were ready to proceed again.

The balky system finally ran in full-power tests, but it got too hot to touch, drew too much power (100 amps), and stopped after a minute or two. Theorizing too much resistance, we installed bigger cables and cleaned connections. We had no better luck, but we were confident that our cables were fine.

As we struggled for enlightenment, we imagined a hidden circuit or mystery box, but by an arduous process of elimination we settled on the idea of being overloaded.

We pulled the boat out of the water and replaced the new three-bladed prop with the original two-bladed prop. This didn't fix our problem, but it did cost a pretty penny and added a vibration since the old prop was out of balance. The only good news was that we also discovered a missing lock pin on the prop shaft, so we could have lost the prop while sailing, which is considered a really bad thing in the middle of a shipping channel.

This was just silly. We were stranded, but we didn't know what the problem was. We had expected to leave the boat works weeks before for our new slip in Baltimore.

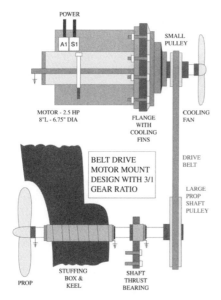

I took the controller to the golf cart repair shop and they certified that the controller and the motor were just fine, with no problems they could detect.

The system's power drain and heat generation were much too high, but we could find no shorts or a clear suspicion. Every test assured us that the motor, the controller, and the other components were on spec.

It still seemed that the system was overloaded, so in desperation, we decided to change the gear ratio to 3/1 with a V-belt drive to unload it further, a complete redesign of the motor mounting system. I pulled the motor the fifth time and designed anew. While

The new motor mount design places the electric motor above the drive shaft and uses pulleys and belts to transmit torque and power to the propeller.

apart, I took the motor to a repair shop. As the helper put it on the workbench, the owner listened offhandedly to my explanation of a golf cart motor on a boat. He shook his head knowingly as I detailed how we set it up.

As I babbled, he pointed at the lead and the helper placed wires to that and the metal case. As I added useless details, he pointed at the post. As the leads touched, a spotlight flashed overhead. With a bright light thrown on the subject, so to speak, he interrupted my dissertation.

"Dead short!"

A smile parted his here-to-fore grim countenance. He preempted my analysis with, "Heats up fast and uses a lot of juice, doesn't she?"

The vertical motor mount was heavy, hard to handle, and almost impossible to install while lying on my back in high humidity and 90-degree temperatures in a tiny space under the cockpit with little light.

"Well, yeah . . . ." I stumbled and mumbled, trying to explain the hard work, hours of diagnosis, confusion, elusive problems. It couldn't be a simple short.

He escorted me out, "Stop back Tuesday, I'll have it fixed." I drove away in shock, thinking, is that all there is? Ten, maybe 12 seconds of work and they diagnosed the problem, even before I could tell them what was wrong. Of all the nerve! At least they could have pretended it was hard. The good news was that there really was something wrong, and it was not black magic haunting us. The bad news was that I had wasted so much time and energy.

The small short in an insulator around a lead in the motor casing was fixed the next day, and they explained that such shorts might not show up in low-voltage or low-amperage testing, but they were testing with 120 VAC which always finds them. That sounded credible, so I asked for more advice.

They confirmed the wisdom of the 3/1 gear reduction system and sold me the pulleys for the belt drive and a cooling fan. I went home, grateful for experts and practical knowledge, remembering, "Book learnin' ain't all it's cracked up to be."

The new design was a radical departure from the old one, and it forced a rethink of the drive system. The design uses the same golf cart motor mounted above the prop shaft with a 3/1 pulley ratio and a V-belt drive. The motor faces forward, above the shaft, with the rear mount bolted to a cross-beam on the rudder post. A pulley and belt-drive system couples the motor and the prop shaft, with mounts to adjust angles and tension.

The drive compartment was restructured and the airflow was rerouted. The wires ran to different locations and the controls fit differently. Each detail led into a number of other changes that caused more changes.

I machined more cooling fins into the flange for better heat dispersion. This doubled the surface on the front of the flange, and with the fan, enhanced the cooling. A grate over the area assures nobody can jam things into the fan, pulleys, or belt, or touch it while in operation.

The bottom of the flange has two adjustable stainless rods bolted into it to support it. The rods also move the motor relative to the shaft for belt adjustment.

Installing the new drive system with the rebuilt motor and the over/under configuration was a nightmare because access was restricted by the drains

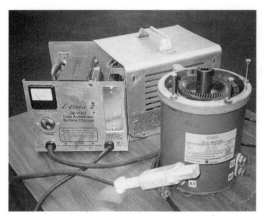

The battery charger in the lazarette with a water shield uses 120-VAC shore power to charge both 36-VDC battery banks through a bank switch.

and tanks. The space was too small for an oversized man to hold an 80-pound motor while bolts, braces, springs, lights, and tools were manipulated.

What might have been a few hours' work took three days of tortuous visits into a claustrophobic space in 90-degree heat, ending with the nauseating job of painting. What I needed was a teenager—someone small enough, smart enough, and silly enough to do the job. I ran out of them years ago, and the new crop of grandchildren wouldn't be ready for a while, so I did it myself.

It took a bit of messing about, but with these changes, the drive system seemed more comfortable, the current draw was reduced considerably, and heat generation dropped somewhat. Two pulley changes permitted us to tune it a bit, so the boat could move around three knots fairly well without getting too hot or drawing too much juice (maximum 90 amps). A half-dozen changes and tests in and out of the harbor assured us we had something that was workable, but slow.

The motor is mounted so it can't vibrate or twist. The two adjustable vertical struts are on springs and rubber shocks to keep tension on the belt and absorb vibration. The rear mount bolts to a beam with rubber mounts. The fan helps cool the engine and exhaust air is vented onto the controller in the lazarette. Since the motor faces forward, the power leads were reversed so the prop turns the right way.

At times the fix was as simple as a slipping V-belt, but we had so many problems that everything was more difficult and confusing than it needed to be. We continued to fix each thing, take short trial runs, change and adjust things until it seemed better. Weeks slipped by as we fought our way past problems, taking longer and with less confidence than we should have. As summer slipped away, we were able to take longer trial runs. We cautiously left for a whole weekend and everything seemed to be working correctly, though it was very slow.

Finally, after six long weeks and four more removals and remountings, it all worked. We left on a shakedown cruise and headed for our new (prepaid) slip down near Baltimore. Even with the vibrating prop, it was quiet and we were quite pleased with our new system. Two hours into the trip, as we began to relax, the motor made a whining-screeching sound. It seized up solidly and was too hot to touch. It was deader 'n a doornail.

We were miles down the river and we hardly had the heart to turn around. We hoisted the sails and explored the area instead. When we could avoid it no longer, we sailed back and dropped the hook near the gas dock. A friend in a dinghy (with internal combustion power) towed us into the marina. After weeks of excuses and delays, this event was more than just embarrassing.

Our neighbors got a chuckle from our disaster, but the idea of extracting and reinstalling the motor a sixth time was more than I could bear. Mentally, I resorted to Scarlett's line from *Gone with the Wind,* "I'll think about that tomorrow," and I went home.

Days later, presented with the charbroiled motor, experts assured me that the only thing wrong was that it was a 30-minute service motor, and in an hour, it burned up.

So, other than cost, lost time, inconvenience, and embarrassment it was just fine, right?

I wonder if age and corrosion further degraded the used golf cart motor that sat in a humid basement for three years during the restoration? In hindsight, I knew that it had overheated a number of times during our trial runs, and I guess this longer run was simply the last straw.

The development of an electric propulsion system had been a nasty experience for months. We were delayed by a variety of electrical and mechanical problems, lack of documentation and instrumentation, corrosion and age problems, gear ratios, and a 30-minute service motor (not including wasted time and installation glitches). I could consider it a character-building opportunity, but I feel that my character can't be bad enough to justify such extreme measures.

In hindsight, we probably found the hardest way to do the job. We not only did the work ourselves, but we did the engineering with used components.

Our neighbors at the Bay Boat Works had a laugh at our expense when we were towed back in after our motor burned up. They couldn't resist sharing their mirth and invested a lot of ingenuity coming up with the key to help. The cardboard key fit prominently on top of the lazarette hatch directly to where it could connect to the propeller. We were pleased, in a Christian kind of way, that we could bring cheer to the hearts of others as they tortured us.

It was fortuitous as well, because we were certainly not in good humor. However, after our experiences, we were so desperate that even this idea was starting to look good.

We considered a new continuous service motor, but our confidence in golf cart conversions was shattered. Skeptically, we found a new marine motor and then designed and built another drive mounting system.

> *When it comes to electric drive systems and boats,*
> *we can say with a great deal of confidence that*
> *golf carts should stay on dry land.*

20

GUNKHOLING WITH CORK DECKS

The Art of Gunkholing is based on doing nothing constructively, and it is practiced nowhere better than on the Chesapeake Bay.

Gunkholing has rules: Wave pleasantly as new gunkholers arrive. If they speak, respond generously. Perhaps note that they are "driving a very shiny bathtub" or some such nicety. As they seek a spot to anchor, help by standing on your foredeck growling when they get too close and smiling as they pull away to an acceptable distance. If they run aground, be sure to be down below lest they enroll you to help get them unstuck.

As soon as your sunscreen is in position, set up cheese, crackers, and wine for all to see how cool and sophisticated you are. Shooting champagne bottle corks onto a neighbor's deck is in bad taste, but popping it noisily after their lights go out is excellent one-upmanship.

However, rain pouring through the decks onto my berth in the middle of the night can put a damper on the gunkholing ambiance.

Following tradition, we rebuilt and restored *Rose*'s white cedar deck in 1998. We were ecstatic with the results. However, in three years, we redid the caulk three times and it still leaked like a sieve.

We hoped that being in the water with high humidity all the time might cure the problem. After all, the plank hull is built the same way. If the deck sealed after she was in the water, then we would try one more repair. If not, we needed an alternative.

However, the planks dried out faster in the sun and the change between wet and dry caused the caulking to split at every seam. A single-planked deck moves and changes shape under the duress of weather and movement of the boat. The sun may drive the surface up to 100 to 120 degrees Fahrenheit on a summer day, and the dried wood can shrink by as much as 15 percent. However, a dowsing by a thunderstorm can cause the wood to swell 15 percent.

Add some bouncing in a seaway and people moving, and it is amazing that decks seal at all.

We had no confidence we could do the caulking better a fourth time, nor that it would change the outcome if we did. Since we were done with the restoration and were in the water, we would not rip the cabin off and build plywood decks. We needed something less intrusive, so we debated epoxy on the planks, fiberglass, canvas over planks, and canvas over plywood over the planks.

Canvas over the planks was the most traditional idea. We even bought canvas, but then a knowledgeable person pointed out that the planks would still move and that the canvas would tear and crack at the joints within a year or so. They insisted that decks must be covered with plywood before laying canvas. We were confused and frustrated. Each idea had disadvantages, but another massive effort with new (for us) techniques did not appeal.

We popped more than a few corks as we debated the problem. This led to a discovery: Cork! It is fire-, water-, rot-, and bug-resistant with natural oils that minimize deterioration. It insulates well and is soft and resilient with a nonskid surface.

We pulled Rose before redoing the decks. Scaffolds surround the boat next to a large 4x16-foot setup table, which is needed to lay out, cut, and fit the 100-foot roll of 1/4-inch cork, before bedding it in 5200 caulk on the deck.

The soles of boat shoes were often made of cork, and the decks of famous vessels such as the *Titanic* and the *Hindenburg* were cork. (I was reluctant to point this out—perhaps *Rose* should not be in such company.) Cork was our answer.

Everyone has noticed that as soon as you have a good idea, you suddenly see everyone is doing it?

As we researched, we discovered that cork is a new trend in deck surfaces for the most expensive vessels, and quotes ran as high as $100 per square foot to install these exotic deck coverings.

We found a local supplier who sold us 4x50-foot rolls of 1/4-inch cork sheathing, and we were able to do the job ourselves. We pulled the boat and surrounded her with scaffolds so we could reach across the deck without getting on it. We removed hardware and deck fittings, filled holes, and sanded the surface smooth.

The cork is flexible, but it will rip or break

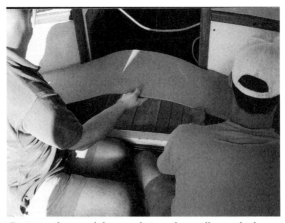

Curing took several days, and since the caulk was thick, some places under the cork took weeks to fully cure. The cork aged to a gray color. We preferred the original tan color, so we sanded it and stained it with Thompson's wood sealer and it looks great.

if it is twisted or bent too far. To make handling easier, we built a flat 16-foot table with plywood and sawhorses for layout and trim. Sharp utility knives cut cork pieces that were glued to the deck to fit against each other. Contact cement was recommended, but it has little working time and we created a mess when we tried to use it.

We had better success with 5200 caulk, which gave us plenty of working time at a considerable expense. The 5200 created a flexible layer that bridged the joints and let the cork work naturally.

Since it was our first experience using cork, we could have done it better. We tried to use sheets that were too large, so it was a messy job that required more hands than we had. As we went along, we did cut the sheets into somewhat smaller sizes.

We struggled with the cork's lack of dimensional stability. The cork does not stay the same size for long. You can also stretch and distort it easily. This is fine once it is attached to a deck that changes shape, but it is a problem for installers.

This problem leaped out at us the first full day of work. We assembled a large crew, created paper templates of the entire deck, and carefully cut and finished each template into a perfect fit. Then we cut the cork to fit the templates perfectly and laid them all out on the worktable for installation the next day.

The next day, we cheerfully organized ourselves and began the laying process, only to discover that every piece of cork was too small, though the templates still fit perfectly. Then, in the process of laying it and rolling it out, it stretched to be larger than the spot it was going into. Now our problem was too short one way and too long another way.

The larger the piece of cork, the more dimensional instability haunted us. What had seemed to be a 15-minute job often slipped into hours before a piece was fitted correctly, smoothed out, and ready for weights to hold it in place while the 5200 cured.

Even then we were not safe. The cork tended to slide, and we could not stand on it to lay the next piece because it might change shape. The laying process went slowly, and it took three weekends to get it right before we put her back in the water, but much of this was due to the learning curve.

We let it cure a while, then went around and trimmed the edges with a straightedge and a utility knife. We put tape on the cork and wood, and then finished off the edges with tan-colored 5200 in all the joints. This touch is crucial for a good-looking job.

Once this was set and cured, we sanded the surface with 120-grit sandpaper with an oscillating sander to eliminate high spots and nasty edges. Next we sealed it with a caramel-colored deck sealer that matched the cork color.

If you do this to your decks, I would suggest a slightly different approach than we took. I would cut 1/4-inch marine plywood pads for each piece of deck hardware. Clean, sand, and finish them nicely, then glue them to the deck with some waterproof bedding material. Screw the deck hardware down to hold it until the bedding cures.

Trim the cork to fit around the pad, place a piece of plywood larger than the pad on top, and screw the hardware onto the temporary brace. After the bedding material cures, remove the brace and hardware. Trim everything, fill the edge so it is finished, then attach the hardware permanently.

I might use smaller pieces with some creative-looking joints that make a nice pattern to match the deck and hardware placement. We created some problems we would avoid if we ever did it again. This is an art, and artists need practice. We simply cannot expect perfection the first time. (Hint: Help somebody else do their boat, then do yours.)

However, the investment was reasonable, and I recommend that anyone consider this alternative, especially those facing the same plank deck problem we had. Final investment: $210 for cork, $250 for 5200 caulk, and $100 for miscellaneous items, plus two weekends (8 man-days) to do the work.

The cork seems traditional in appearance, and it looks as if it had naturally always been there. It is waterproof, soundproof, and not too cold or too hot, a welcome to my bare feet. Cork looks great and works well. What more can one ask?

Our big regret was the loss of the beautiful wood decks, especially after all the work we had done. We could have put cork over the old ugly decks in the first place and it would have worked just as well, saving thousands of dollars and many hours of work. I can't swear (yet) that cork is that rare idea that works for years, but after two years, it seems perfect.

We were spoiled by the performance of our last boat (a Gemini 32-foot

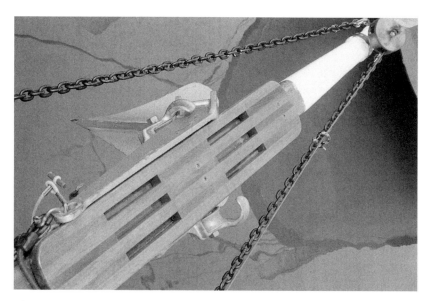

The teak platform was made from 1x1-inch strips with stainless through-bolts and mounted on the bowsprit for safety and convenience.

catamaran) and are dismayed by less-than-optimal performance in *Rose.* This inflated standard caused frustration and debate as we tried to make tradeoffs for this vessel.

Rose is a big 25-foot boat, with an 8-foot beam and a gross weight of 6,000 pounds. How strong do blocks have to be? How big should anchors and chains be? Such issues beg easy answers, so we faced the shakedown cruise with apprehension. However, there were lots of items to tend to, though the only major problems came from some bad rigging and the bowsprit-anchoring system invited trouble. This was high on our priority list for finishing, and several problems became a major project:

- too much manual handling of anchors, lines, and chains;
- anchors were inconvenient, unattractive, and cluttered the forward deck; and
- bowsprit was dangerous to stand, sit, or move about on in any sea.

A plow anchor with a curved stem hangs from the bowsprit, whereas a Danforth with a straight stem must be stowed on deck. However, a plow as good as a Danforth is larger and required a new anchor-roller to handle it. A side advantage is that a plow anchor should work better on some bottoms. We found a more substantial, bronze dual roller that needed customization to work with the plow anchor. A thick teak plate on either side of the bowsprit acts as braces for the roller and positions the anchor properly when it is stowed.

I made an interesting anchor capstan with wood and a 2-inch winch mounted on the bowsprit. Raising and lowering the anchor is straightforward if I sit on the forward hatch and tie the lines off on the bollards, even in the heaviest seas.

I designed a bowsprit platform for better footing and safety. It is half the length of the bowsprit, but provides a nice step or seat halfway between the deck and the tip of the bowsprit. It is made of 1-inch square 30-inch long teak strips glued and bolted together and varnished. I screwed it on top of the bowsprit with stainless spacers to elevate it to avoid buildup of dirt and moisture to cause rot. It looks nice and works great, while also allowing me to move on the bowsprit safely.

Good anchoring is crucial; nothing makes one feel so insecure as waking in the darkness to see something that does not look right. We have three anchors onboard *Rose*: The big plow on the bowsprit for most anchoring, a large Danforth in the focs'le as a backup, and a small mushroom in the cockpit for swim stops, not overnight or with winds or tides. I painted the ground tackle with Rustoleum "hammered bronze." There are two anchor line setups, 100 feet of 1-inch line with a 20-foot chain for light work, and 200 feet of chain for heavy work. Either setup can be used with either anchor.

Amidst shore lights and reflections, boaters may not see a masthead light, so we hang a second anchor light on the boom, which moves energetically to catch attention. At bedtime we have a routine: run out long anchor chain, drop floating cushion behind, set up boarding ladder and bug screens, hang extra anchor light, plug in 1/2-mile beam. Our ritual stems from experience, not theory.

The 1/2-mile beam saved us several times. One night on the Bohemia River, as I enjoyed a beautiful summer's night, I heard a John Phillip Souza march getting louder as the source came closer. Curious, I saw a brightly lit motor-yacht coming up the river, then turning toward our anchorage. The sound got louder as he stormed in and turned toward us. Souza almost drowned out the diesels, and lights went on as noise awoke sleepers in nearby vessels.

I aimed my beam's 1,000,000-candlepower into the eyes of the inebriated helmsman. Shocked, he turned, so close everyone was thrown out of their bunks by his wake. He missed a dozen anchored boats, and ran onto the beach at full speed. As the crunching noises of propellers collapsing under the power of the diesels and the weight of the boat on the rocky beach subsided, the vessel lurched over at a list and settled. Moments later, the music died to a cheer from everyone anchored in the cove.

Cheryl has a tradition of falling overboard. She had some noteworthy splashdowns in Baltimore Inner Harbor and the Vickers Canal in London, but any place will do. Climbing back up in style means a good ladder. Our curved, hull-fitting, folding mahogany ladder is a gem. We found it in a flea market and rebuilt it with teak steps and bronze hinges. The hinged steps fold flat between the sides, forming a unit (6 feet long x 6 inches x 3 inches) small enough to stow on the cabin top, or in hooks over the berth. The toe-rail and bumper rails create a mounting for the bronze straps. Once opened and snapped into its designated spot, it cannot fold up.

An important part of gunkholing is the dinghy for grandchildren and exploring the Bay. It also transports creatures, pocketbooks, and any other small items. Cheryl has a small, green dink that is appropriately named *Thorn,* a Walker Bay 8. This fine little craft is made of hard plastic and does the job.

I have always seen mechanical things as primarily functional in nature. However, the experience with Rose leads me to believe that the merger of utility and beauty is an integral part of the human experience.

The next time you open a bottle of wine, fondle the cork for a second, think about your leaking decks, and consider the possibilities. Then, get out there and do some serious gunkholing.

21

A GAFF FOR *ROSE*

Everyone loves those beautiful boats of yesteryear with their magnificent gaff rigs. These rigs were the choice for ships, workboats, fishing boats, and small boats for centuries. The lower, wider rig looks and handles very different than taller, thinner rigs.

The four-sided mainsail keeps the center of gravity and force low, reducing heel and enhancing power. It is a good design for going downwind or off-wind, but it is not so good to pinch into the wind.

Rose weighs in at a hefty 6,000 pounds, the hull is full (8-foot beam on a 21-foot waterline), and her straight keel reaches down less than 4 feet. This design gives *Rose* the image of a tub; she's more slow and stable than fast and frivolous. We intended to do the best we could with this design and accept no compromises on the rigging.

However, when we started restoring *Rose*, we had never seen a gaff rig up close, much less sailed one. As we disassembled the worn and battered pile that would become *Rose*, we were mystified by the parts and lines. I cautiously labeled each, so I might get her back together later. This was fortunate, since it took five years to rebuild and restore the boat, and I had forgotten it all by the time we rigged it.

We knew that eventually we needed new sails and lines, but we didn't know what we should have. With little clue of how the sails would work, we planned to get new sails and redo the rig after we learned how to sail with it.

The rig has a gaff boom (top) and main boom (bottom) above and below the mainsail, designed to stretch the sail between them. Two halyards control the gaff boom, and thereby the mainsail.

We faced the shakedown cruise apprehensively, but I slowly learned to use the halyards, (as in "Haul yards") to raise and lower the gaff boom and mainsail. The main halyard attaches to the forward end of the gaff boom at a yoke around the mast, while the peak halyard attaches to the middle. The halyards permit the sail-trimmer to control the shape of the sail stretched between the booms.

Handling them is okay in perfect conditions, but how often does that happen? We often raise or lower sails near harbor while being flung about by boats competing for the coveted Giant Wake Award. Contenders hammer a hapless sailor caught in the middle, so I stay under power a little longer to avoid getting beat up where the contest is most vicious. This also frees up my hands for appropriate gesturing (cheering on the Giant Wake contenders).

Stepping mast into the mast step through the deck collar. Halyard setup, boom yokes, and sail hoops are unique to gaff rigs and it took a lot of planning and double-checking to get it all right before the mast was lowered into place. Even then, we climbed the mast or hoisted someone to the top a dozen times before we finally got everything correct.

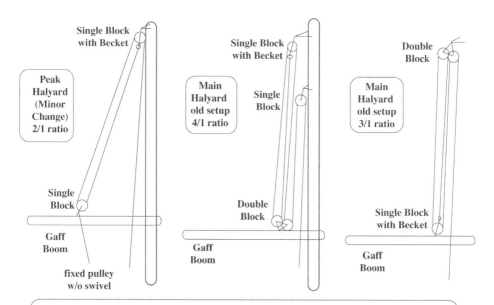

Rigging the two main halyards of the gaff rig to prevent jamming and fouling to get both to work in unison

I try to organize the raising or lowering process to be more predictable so I can check for problems. Cheryl, as the pilot, is buried under cloth when I drop the mainsail, but topping off the experience with a heavy wood spar upset her to no end. I fixed that problem fast, along with other minor handling and rigging problems, and we did a lot better in the next 100 miles.

Even after I stopped dropping the gaff boom on Cheryl, it took lots of messing to handle the mainsail. The gaff boom jammed on the mast end and let the free end sag, straining and breaking the yoke. I was frustrated by a rig simple and safe enough to be handled by fishermen trying to do a job.

All this trouble did not make sense until I saw we were suffering a triple-whammy, the main halyard jammed when lowered, the peak halyard twisted when raised, and the halyards did not work in unison. Most of the work of raising and lowering the main was moving lines, not moving the gaff and sail.

After a lot of fussing and changes, wasted fixes, and more analysis, I realized that the halyards were improperly rigged to start and the lines were a mess at the masthead. This was bothersome, and since we were concerned about the rigging and lacking confidence, we hired expensive riggers who ignored the designer's drawings and made a mess of the rigging.

Gaff Boom Yoke Design

bolt
holes

6 in
diameter

4 in
wide

TOP VIEW

6 in
diameter

<< 24 in long >>

1.5 in
thick

side view

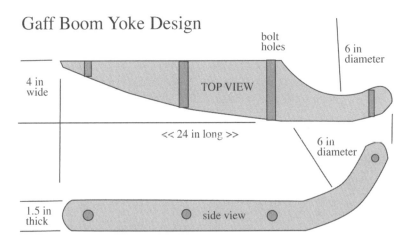

The gaff boom yoke was twisted and broken by bad rigging. I made this new one with two matching pieces of white oak, as in the drawing below.

Nine bronze chainplates (two each side for shrouds, one each side for running backstays, one either side for the bowsprit side chains, and one at the waterline for the lower bowsprit chain) attach with silicon bronze bolts through the hull into oak braces or through the keel.

The peak halyard block swiveled as the gaff boom was raised, causing a twisted mass of rope, which stopped it from going higher. This made no sense, but an expert from Fawcett's Marine explained that rope has a biased structure and pressure naturally untwists the rope. Since the pulley rotated, it twisted the rope around itself.

The 65-foot peak halyard has a 2/1 ratio. It loops over a masthead block, around a block on the gaff, and then up to a becket on the masthead. All I did to correct the problem was put a fixed pulley on the gaff, which prevents twisting and binding. Then the halyard rotated enough to compensate for the bias and the induced twist. It was a simple enough concept that seems counterintuitive.

The 80-foot main halyard had a 4/1 ratio that jammed easily and had more power than needed for the boom and sail. It looped over a single block close to the masthead, then down to a double block on the gaff, then back up to a single block partway down the mast, then back to the double block on the gaff, then up to a becket on a single block. It also twisted around itself since the runs caused the lines to lie on top of each other.

I redid the setup to fit the design and re-rigged it myself. We replaced the main halyard with a 65-foot line with a 3/1 ratio that loops over a double block at the masthead, then down to a single block on the gaff yoke, back up and over the double block, and ends at a becket on the block on the gaff yoke.

This is simpler with cleaner runs that are less likely to jam, with plenty of power for the weight of the gaff and sail. This results in faster and safer sail-handling and I am less likely to get in trouble in choppy seas. If this continues to work well, I might take the main halyard to a 2/1 ratio (like the peak halyard) so they work in unison.

The running backstays were a concern; I had never used them before. (I thought "running backstays" was a football play.) They seemed complex and dangerous, so I researched them as we rebuilt. They attached to eyebolts in the deck, which had significant damage and had to be replaced. I added a chainplate that simplified the rig and put the stress in a stronger, more convenient location.

This worked well, and we had no problems with the running backstays. They are only used when running dead downwind, and we have survived two accidental jibes without damage, so they are hardier than expected.

Lazy jacks gather in the sail, booms, and lines as the mainsail is lowered. They are not really a part of the standing or running rigging, but as a safety item they are crucial as the large mainsail, long boom, and gaff boom flail about in a seaway. It took a lot of time to get them in adjustment and working properly. They look fine since for each side I found bronze contraptions with two small pulleys that connect all the lines.

We struggled with reefing. The jib is on roller furling, which works full-in or full-out. We also had several jams and refittings before we could get comfortable with it. It does require that we keep it well lubricated and maintain some tension on the lines to avoid the roller getting bound up. Once we figured all that out, it seemed to work pretty well.

The mainsail should provide the primary driving force for a gaff-rig anyhow, but this can be a real challenge since the boom is long, and hanging on to it while a dozen ties are properly fastened to complete the reef is a long and painstaking process. Our sailmaker suggested a set of lines that act like slab reefing. Then the ties are used to bundle up excess sail material. It is not a great answer, but it is better than getting thrown overboard by a misbehaving boom in a heavy sea.

As we started sailing, we were expecting the worse. Fortunately, once the lines were rerouted correctly, the rig was easier than expected to use, and the boat sailed well. Despite the problems, by the end of the shake-down cruise, we felt confident enough to order the new sails. These fit the original designer's specs, with minor changes to the mainsail.

The new sails did get rid of my excuses to avoid making rigging changes, so now I had to find more bronze and climb the mast, a task I religiously avoid. We all know sailors should joyfully spring to the masthead anytime the vessel demands it, but my no-longer-buns-of-steel refuse to make the trip up the mast as in yesteryear.

Secretly, I created a rope and wood ladder that rolls into a small bundle. Attached to a halyard, I can haul it aloft with the bitter ends of two side-ropes tied to deck cleats, with bungee cords attached to the stays to stabilize it. It's not glamorous, but I should be able to singlehanded repairs if necessary.

The theory sounded good, but as I started to climb, the ladder settled with a lot of creaking and groaning. It stretched into an elongated structure with steps so far apart I couldn't get beyond the fourth step. Apparently my immense presence caused this embarrassing occurrence, but I blamed it on the poor rope in the construction.

I hid the evidence and recruited my friend Al to haul me up in a bosun chair. The look on his face attested to the strain on the lines, winch, and shoulders. Despite the sounds, I rerigged the halyards, but it will be a long time before I do it again.

Standing rigging on a wood boat is a bigger issue than I thought when we started this project. The mast should be canted aft 3 to 10 degrees, with blocks hammered into the deck collar and the mast step. The bowsprit is also standing rigging, a spar sticking out toward the front instead of up. The bowsprit is tuned with a chain to the keel at the water-line, two side chains, and the forestay to the mast with the shrouds attached to the chainplates along the sides.

The bronze chainplates attach with five 3/8-inch silicon bronze bolts to white-oak braces in the hull. They are a key part of the structure and distribute the force of the sails through the rigging to the hull.

Even if it is perfectly tuned, the hull and rigging works as it is sailed and hammered around in a seaway, and the rig slips out of tune. Good performing sails require a well-tuned rig, but the shrouds and stays on *Rose* seem to be lazy. We tuned the rigging on *Rose* when we installed the mast and sails in June, then sailed the boat for perhaps 50 miles, then tuned again in October.

We did another tuning in April 2002, just before we left on our shakedown cruise. However, after 300 miles of sailing, the side shrouds could be shaken by hand. The mast and bowsprit moved visibly a few inches at the ends and leaks sprung around the mast-to-deck fitting. Some of the play we found was the result of the driest summer in years, which causes wood to shrink and warp.

Excessive play in the standing rigging can be dangerous. Stresses are placed on one fitting, shroud, or chainplate, rather than spread over the rigging. Such forces can be more than a given component is designed to handle. This results in wear or failure, which can cascade failures or cause a catastrophe.

I understand why wood sailing ships had simple tuning blocks for their shrouds. It is not just ropes stretching, but the vessel changes shape. They probably tuned the rigging each time they set sail. With this new insight, I will check the rigging each time we sail and plan to adjust the tuning at least once a month in the future.

Now, we have a good gaff rig for many years, as long as we pay attention and plan ahead for sail changes and reefing. We started out knowing nothing, and we will keep changing things as we go, but now we can learn how to really sail this boat.

After trial runs and a shakedown cruise, we still felt she was not as fast as she should be and did not point as well as we had hoped. We ordered new sails, but a major contributor had to be the oversized propeller. This showed itself at the worst possible times—at low speeds in light winds and when trying to point into a headwind. Obviously something had to be done with the prop.

These rigging changes, tuning, and adjustments yielded a decent rig. We will keep learning and changing things as we go, but this round of changes promised to get us into shape. We were feeling pretty good about *Rose* as our first season of sailing settled into history.

The scariest thing about this story is that now we are considered experts.
Makes you wonder, doesn't it?

*

22

MORE POWER

When we started restoring *Rose,* we had never sailed a gaff rig. Atkin, the designer, wrote "Sails are Power" on the design drawings, reinforcing the need to deal with all aspects of the sails. We needed new sails, but we were concerned since they were expensive and we didn't know what we should have.

I felt a cutter rig with two foresails was a more classic setup and perhaps easier to balance in a variety of wind conditions. However, the boat did okay with a sloop rig for nearly 40 years, and the idea of a roller-furling jib controlled from the cockpit has appeal versus the idea of clambering out onto a bowsprit every time a jib needs to be set.

We decided to get new sails and redo the rig after we learned how to sail her as she was designed. We had the old sails inspected, repaired, and cleaned. Then we faced the shakedown cruise with apprehension. However, in the first 100 miles we learned that the boat sailed okay if we could figure out how to handle it right.

I learned to use two lines (halyards) to raise and lower the gaff boom and mainsail. These stretch the sail between the gaff and main booms to shape the sail for conditions. However, we had a bad time with furling and reefing. As we got details worked out to do the tasks properly, the rig proved satisfactory.

The jib is on a roller-furling setup, which only seems to work properly full-in or full-out. In between, the twist on the sail is transmitted upward, opening it, so the bottom is partially furled and sail-shape is trashed. Reefing a roller-furling jib is difficult, and the mainsail is the primary driving force for a gaff rig anyhow, so reefing the jib is not critical.

However, the furling and reefing setup on the sails is pretty important since a fully raised sail can overpower the boat in the wrong winds. Disregarding control and safety issues, just the physical effort alone may be impossible in heavy winds. (We can't lash down the sheets until the furling or reefing is complete, so the sheets cannot help control things.)

The boom is long (17 feet), and hanging on to the boom while ties are fastened to complete the reef is a long process while the boat slams and bangs around, and the boom swings to and fro enthusiastically. I can tie perhaps one reef tie every 30 seconds, so it takes six minutes to tie a dozen ties. Allowing a minute or so to lower the halyard and retighten, and more for the outhaul, cleanup, tightening the mainsheet, and getting back on course, a *quick* reef may take perhaps 10 minutes. One day, we took at least 20 minutes to reef the sails in a brutal blow with the boat rolling 30 degrees on each side in the waves. We had to exhaust a lot of effort to simply hang on. After that, I focused a lot of attention on these two issues. I carefully disassembled the roller-furling jib mechanisms, then cleaned and lubricated them. I also carefully lubed the steel cable of the furling guy. Magically, the roller-furling jib seemed to work much better. This process has been repeated twice, and each time yielded excellent results. It seems that twice-a-year lubrication is critical to this roller-furling system.

In the future, we plan to do the reefs long before they are needed, and in more pleasant circumstances. (It is probably the reef that has been delayed too long that is the most difficult and dangerous one to do.)

Rose was not fast, but off-wind she ran well enough and she was easier to handle than we expected. The roller-furling jib was great, and the main-sail could even be reefed if we gave ourselves enough time. By the end of the shakedown cruise, we felt confident enough to get new sails in the original design with minor changes.

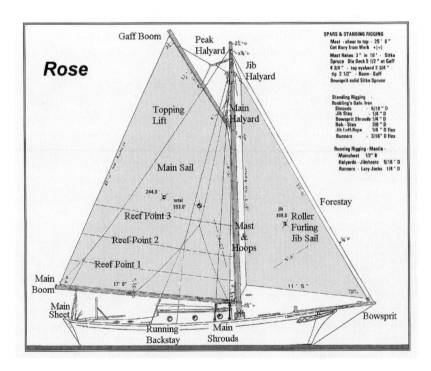

Layout and cutting of Egyptian cream–colored cloth for the roller-furling jib requires exacting overlaps to assure the right curve and fullness in the sail.

Layout and cutting of Oceanus Tanbark cloth for the gaff mainsail takes a lot of space since the foot is almost 18 feet long.

Meade Breese is our selected sailmaker as much for the perfection of his name (it was as if Dickens dreamed it up) as for his attitude and experience with a gaff-rigged boat. He spent extra time and effort helping us with reefing the sails, rerouting lines, and moving hardware to assure that it all worked. The process of making a sail is interesting unto itself, but making one for an older boat is especially challenging. Meade and his wife, Cheryl, provided pictures to show us how it works.

We spoke to him about the reefing issue but didn't get much sympathy. He suggested a powerful pull-down line below the boom, which can also act as a downhaul. We will also add two powerful outhaul and downhaul lines on the boom end, one for each reef point. Together, these should be enough to reef the main without depending on the ties. Then the ties will be used to bundle up excess sail material.

We added two outhaul and downhaul lines on the boom end, one for each reef point. Together, these should be enough to reef the main like slab reefing, without depending on the ties. Then the ties will be used to bundle up excess sail material. He designed the new main accordingly, and hand-sewed the eyes to ease the reefing task. The lines on the outboard end of the boom have been a bit of a hassle since they dangle at the worst times when we are raising or reefing sails. He also placed fewer ties strategically to ease the problems.

The sails fit the designer's specs, but on the mainsail there are no battens and only two reef points instead of three. The design is based on Meade's recommendations and our experience sailing about 300 miles with the old sails.

The new mainsail is made of a tanbark-colored material with the seams running diagonally down from the top toward the back. It is sewn in a classic style with no battens and only two reef points. The jib is made in a lighter material and a pleasant color called "Egyptian cream." The two complement each other with a very European flavor.

Grommets on the corners and reef points are hand-sewn bronze to assure strength and maintain the character of the sails, though the handwork was difficult and expensive.

We were surprised with the amount of time Meade spent measuring and fitting. He spent extra time and effort helping us deal with issues, lines, and hardware to assure that everything worked well. He visited *Rose* five times. His initial visit was for measurements, so we took both sails off and measured every edge of the existing sails as well as the halyards, heights, booms, and everything else he wanted to measure.

I told him about the problems getting the gaff boom to come down because of rigging issues. He looked like I was nuts and hoisted the naked gaff boom up, only to discover it would not come down. He shimmied up the mast, but to my horror, he slid down because of the Pam spray I had put on the mast to make things slide. Incredibly, he shimmied far enough to grab the boom and drag it down. I was embarrassed to admit it was Pam, but I gave him a rag to rub the slimy stuff off his body.

The second visit was nicer, since we installed the new mainsail, and I had already rerigged the main halyards, so things worked better. Fortunately, nobody had to shimmy up the mast again, and he did accept the towel to clean his hands and the mast while working around the hoops and mast.

The third visit he installed the new jib sail, and that was the easiest of all three visits. The pride he showed in his handiwork was richly deserved, as we found out the next weekend, when we had a delightful sail and discovered that new sails make a major difference in the speed and handling of a boat. We had never switched from old to new sails without first changing boats. It was a real eye-opener!

We assured ourselves it was worth every cent when we saw not just how well she sailed, but how well the sails worked and looked. *Rose* is already seen as a bit of tub, but we don't want to be slower than necessary. The issue is balanced performance. We wanted the best we could get with this boat design.

She refuses to go upwind with enthusiasm, but she is better in the pinch. Light-wind performance improved, probably by a full knot in smooth water, with some in moderate to heavy winds. She accelerates

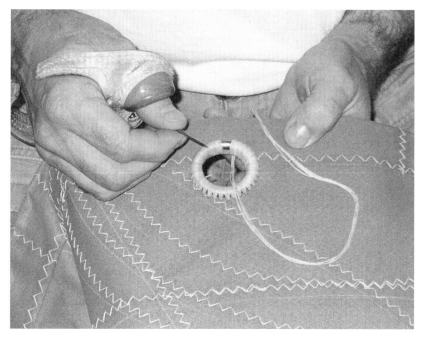

Details count. Hand-stitching bronze rings is difficult and time consuming, but it is necessary for the right look and strength in Rose's traditional sails.

better in most conditions, which makes a big difference while cruising. We are pleased with the performance and the appearance.

The mainsail material, Oceanus Tanbark, is not really red, but it bears a close resemblance to the reddish colors Cheryl selected for the interior cushions, which she called "rose." However, the new sail has another furling problem, which seemed to get worse with time. We returned the sail to Meade and he fixed it. He was worried that the cable was installed upside down (did you know there was an up- and down-side to a stainless steel cable?) That was not the problem, but he promptly replaced the cable with a larger, stiffer cable, and we have had no problems since.

Birds appreciate the sounds of a wood mast, so we get feathered visitors from miles around. All the spiders and birds work hard to make their mark on our sails, deck, and cabin. A sail cover has to fit around halyards, reef lines, lazy jacks, and ties in the gaff rig. However, we can't find an easy alternative, so we had Meade repair an old cover until we could afford a new one.

The new sails make a major difference in the speed and handling of a boat. Of course, once the sails worked properly, we no longer had any excuses for our slow speed other than our incompetence or propeller drag. Unwilling to accept the alternative, we naturally looked around for ways to replace the prop. This impediment showed itself at the worst times—in light winds, and when pointing into a headwind. Our primary concern was sailing performance, but we could not afford any loss of efficiency on the electric drive either. The real issue was overall performance. We want the best balance we could get, based on the boat design, and we are not there yet.

We started out knowing nothing, and we will keep learning and changing things as we go, as soon as we learn how to really sail this boat.

With the new sails, we declared Rose *completed on the outside.*
But as always, there were just a few more things to do.

SILENCE OF THE SEA, PART III:
JUST TOO DUMB TO GIVE UP!

After six weeks of frustration with our electric drive, we left on a shaky shakedown cruise, hoping that nothing else could go wrong. However, two hours into the trip, the motor made a whining-screeching sound and seized up solid. After a humiliating sail back to the marina, we admitted that our faith in golf cart conversions was shattered.

Skeptically, we found a marine motor that looked similar, but cost twice as much, from a reputable marine supplier. Then we had to design and build a new mounting system for the larger, heavier, and more powerful motor. Essentially, we abandoned the golf cart conversion approach and took what we had and started over.

The new 7.5-horsepower motor is slower but more powerful than the 2.5-horsepower motor. It can run up to 350 amps short term or 225 amps continuously, versus the old one at 125 amps for 30 minutes (not continuous). The new motor operates on 36 or 48 VDC, with a built-in fan that circulates air through the motor. Certainly, it would handle our needs.

The final drive design uses a marine electric motor, mounted above the prop shaft with a 2/3 pulley ratio and a V-belt drive. The motor faces forward, above the shaft, with the rear mount bolted to a crossbeam on the rudder post. The mounts are 2-foot long, 3/8-inch, threaded stainless rods with nuts and locking nuts against the mounts to adjust angles and tension. We did use some parts of the second drive system, but the cool machined aluminum flange didn't make it. There is a cooling fan mounted on the shaft and an aluminum shield helps duct the air toward the back, while protecting the tanks and wiring from overheating.

Recalling the horror of the last installation with a smaller, lighter motor, I built an installation rig of handles, pulleys, and cables to get the new motor into place. The assembly holds the motor while bolts and belts are fitted. As a result, installation took four hours and though I had to crawl into the hole six times in 90-degree temperatures, the rig let me install with only minor physical damage to me and the boat.

We tested and messed around with it through four variations to get an acceptable gear ratio of pulleys and belts. The new mount is strong and adjustable to handle belt tension, but with two belts and more power, there is slippage and vibration. There are also some alignment issues and belt noises; our drive was not silent anymore. It ran slowly during the trials, and we had a vibration and a rat's nest of wiring from our diagnostic efforts, but it was working, so we used it to test and refine everything. Later, we remounted and realigned the pulleys at right angles to each other, added an idler pulley, and corrected twist in the assembly when under full power.

When finished, the motor is mounted so it can't vibrate or twist. The two vertical struts are on springs and rubber shocks and are adjustable to keep tension on the belt and absorb vibration. The rear mount is bolted to

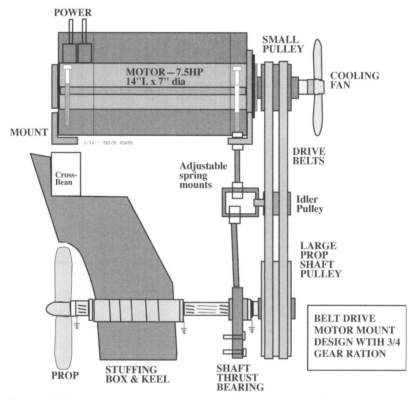

The new 7.5-horsepower motor was mounted in a similar fashion to the last (second) design, but its greater size, weight, and power demanded all new mounting components, dual belts, and plenty of tuning to work right.

a crossbeam. The fan helps cool the engine and exhaust air vents into the lazarette. The motor faces forward, so power leads were reversed so the prop would turn the right way.

In our third engine trial, the drive system ran for 5 1/2 hours, with nominal current draw and tolerable heat. This success let us feel better than we had in weeks, but this newest incarnation had cost us another three weeks of work and $1,200. However, the drive system seemed functional with the new motor and an appropriate gear ratio and double belts and stronger adjustments, so we cleaned it up and wished for the best. Seemingly past the stage that anything else could go wrong, we finished off a few projects, rearranged our schedules, packed up, and left on another shakedown cruise.

Incredibly, we were stopped by a burned out controller at the same spot near Turkey Point. Somehow it didn't surprise us . . . We sailed around in a circle, dropped the hook, seethed for a while, and then sailed back to the marina. The controller worked in slow for final docking, so we were at least saved that humiliation.

We had suspected a problem with the controller, but we were unable to prove it was defective. Research yielded the fact that the golf cart controller can operate at a max level of 225 amps for a short time (i.e.

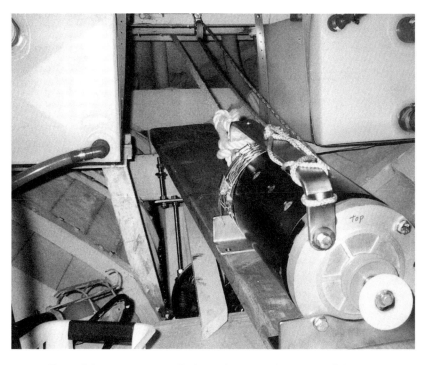

Line, pulley, and the ramp rig to install a larger, heavier, and more powerful motor in the motor compartment

minutes) but it probably won't handle 75 amps for hours without over-heating. In a sense the controller was also not a continuous service device.

Again I ask, can't somebody tell us these things *before* they break? Why should we have to ignore the ads and features lists and examine the specifications with an electrical theory book in one hand and a law book in the other? I was amazed to learn there is no labeling standard for electric motors. One label claims horsepower, another max amperage, another may show continuous service draw. Wiring diagrams may or may not be included. There is no excuse for the misinformation in the electrical industry. In my opinion, it is actually bad for the industry, not just the consumer. If the consumer and mechanics and users of the equipment had the information they need, they could use this technology better and more frequently.

With this perspective, I very carefully researched a new controller and found a good deal on one that was rated for 500 AMPS max and 225 amps continuous. This was twice what we expected full-out, for plenty of safety margin. In addition, it would permit us to upgrade to 48 volts without replacing the motor or the controller. It also has advanced features such as KEY SWITCH INTERLOCK and START ONLY IN NEUTRAL that might be convenient and cost nothing extra.

The original 200-amp controller burned up and was pulled from the lazarette. It was rebuilt with the new controller and beefier parts to match the larger motor.

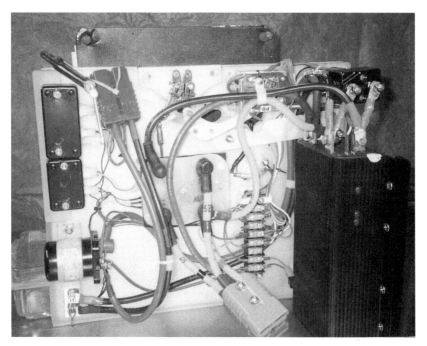

The new, larger 500-amp controller needed a new board, cables, plugs, layout, and retesting in the EDSL.

The new controller is four times as heavy as the old one, twice as big, and creates more heat. I redesigned the circuit board and mounts and discovered that advanced features could be enabled, so we wired those in along with bank switches and a charger circuit, and added a voltmeter-ammeter display (a digital multimeter).

When we were finished, the only thing left from the original board was the key switch and primary solenoid, worth perhaps $50. The only other thing left from the original golf cart installation was the 36-volt charger, worth maybe $300, and quite a poor return for a $1,500 investment and many hours of work. There were so many changes of the cables and wiring and switches and mounts that by any basis, this new system qualified as drive system number four.

The controller calls for a 0-5k ohm potentiometer as a throttle. After so many disappointments, I spent $90 to buy the throttle from Curtis, even though a potentiometer cost $3 at Radio Shack. This avoided building a mount, arms, and harness, sealing it for corrosion and second-guessing whether it might work. However, after installation, the system worked backward.

Jeff, the electrical engineer, and I reread the instructions a half-dozen times, remeasuring, double- and triple-checking. We finally guessed that the two sets of instructions (one for the controller, the other for the

The new motor needs a lot of cooling. A large fan mounts on the front and circulators force air through the armature and windings.

throttle) from the same manufacturer were written by different people: one spoke in terms of resistance and the other in terms of voltage, which are inversely related to each other. This was our only theory, so we disassembled the potentiometer, mounted everything in reverse, and reassembled it to get the system working correctly.

We had to reset the potentiometer to work from 4.5k-0k ohms rather than 0.3k–5k ohms, which is what one set of instructions implied. This meant ripping the controller board out of the vessel and remanufacturing the mount and wiring harness. Incredibly it worked just fine, proving our theory was right. Jeff works in electronics and assures me this is how they do it.

Fortunately, the new board was designed to come in and out easily. We had taken the original out a dozen times, which took about an hour, and twice as long to put in. It was complicated and prone to error and damage the components. The new one takes 10 minutes, and connections are more robust and less likely to break.

Unfortunately, this problem cost another month and $1,000. We were late and far over budget, but pleased with our success in the battle.

Forlorn to have lost the war, we gave up on the shakedown cruise and moving south. We focused on finishing and commissioning and stayed at the Boat Works for one more season.

The conversion to electric propulsion was a nasty experience. We were delayed by bad information, poor diagnosis, and mechanical and electrical problems. Lack of documentation and instrumentation, corrosion, age, gear ratios, and a 30-minute service motor further stalled the project.

Unfortunately, there was little data and few options when we started, though options and sources of information popped up in the four years it took us to finish the restoration.

In hindsight, we probably found the hardest way to do the job. We not only did the work and engineering, but we bought used components. All of these factors seem to guarantee problems. Eventually, we created an acceptable drive system, but I suggest that others use an existing marine system. It would be worth a lot to miss some of the challenges we had.

When all the work came together, we were able to move at a nice speed with good forward/aft and steering maneuverability. We will try the smaller prop, adjust the gear ratio, and perhaps upgrade to a 48-volt battery and charger system, later.

A major contributor to our slow sailing speed was the oversized propeller we were using to optimize the power of the electric drive system. It created a lot of drag; we could see it, feel it, and corroborate it with common sense and any book on propellers and sailboats.

It was a catch-22: the prop slowed us down when sailing; therefore, we use the electric drive more than planned. We could not afford any loss of efficiency on the electric drive either.

We considered reverting back to the original prop, a 16x8-inch, two-bladed bronze affair that had half the drag of the 15x9, three-bladed prop we were using. A folding prop would be even less efficient as an electric drive unit and generally a poor performer in harbor where we needed it the most, though it would reduce the drag while sailing.

The best solution would be some kind of feathering prop, but they seemed to be expensive and complicated. The KiwiProp was the most attractive of those, since it would provide minimal drag while sailing and maximum push while motoring. It only had two negatives: it looked rather high-tech, unlike the traditional-looking bronze, and it cost far more than we had planned to spend after all the money we spent on the new sails. The real issue, though, was overall performance. Flustered and out of money, we simply put the older two-bladed prop back on for this season.

In the future, we may upgrade to a 48-VDC system. We might add more 6-VDC batteries (though space and weight is an issue) or wait until it is time to replace the 6-VDC batteries with 8-VDC batteries. We plan to pull *Rose* in the spring to repaint the bottom and hull and check everything over. This would be a good opportunity to replace the prop and realign the motor and drive system; maybe we will even consider upgrading to 48 volts then.

We were pleased with the system, but we learned to live with its limitations as well. After years of work, we were facing that moment when it all was supposed to come together and we would find out if we had a usable boat or an attractive basket case. Our apprehension was as high as our anticipation as we closed her up for another winter.

A perfect morning is a flat sheen of water, a whisper of breeze, and a warm cup of java as we quietly glide off into a great sunrise. With such a dream in mind, we began the conversion of a traditional 25-foot sloop into an electric auxiliary.

In hindsight, I am reminded that pioneers are the ones with the arrows in their backs.

OPERATING CHARACTERISTICS
OF ELECTRIC DRIVE SYSTEM

The operating characteristics of an electric drive system are unique to the installation and the vessel. Here are the charts and rules we created for our system. To create these charts, use a voltmeter to measure battery charge and an ammeter to measure the rate of use. We considered slow as 15 amps (about 2 knots), half speed as 25 amps (about 3 knots), fast as 45 amps (about 4 knots), and full speed as 75 amps (about five knots) based on our boat and drive system.

ELECTRIC DRIVE RULES
OF OPERATION:

We did several trial runs with a careful log tracking voltage, amperage, time, and speed. With this data we derived the charts and based rules of operation in this table. These will probably *not* apply exactly to your vessel and drive system, but it may help as guidelines.

• Figure about 1 horsepower per 1,000 pounds of displacement to reach an acceptable cruising speed. A 6,000-pound boat needs at least 6 horsepower;
• Lower your expectations. A good cruising speed is only 75 percent of hull speed; a 25-foot boat has a 6-knot hull speed but a 4.5-knot cruising speed;
• Approaching hull speed eats power, drains batteries, and overworks the system. Use "full out" only in emergencies;
• We go much farther at slower speeds than at faster ones. The difference is dramatic: 10 miles at 5 knots or 20 miles at 3 knots;
• Plan shorter runs. A good setup gives a nice cruising speed for a half-dozen hours at best, so why get frustrated with unrealistic expectations? and
• Plan to operate as a sailboat. A motor is an option for occasional situations. The motor is not an alternative to sailing—it is an auxiliary.

Operating Range Left Chart shows the projected operating range left based on the battery bank voltage level and the operating speed (two banks will each have their own range).

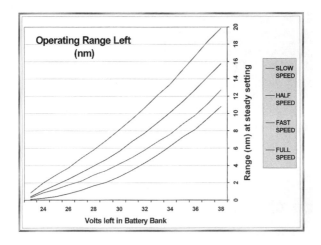

CONCLUSION:
Range goes up dramatically as speed goes down. If we run at full speed the range is about 9 miles on a bank, but at slow speed, we go almost 18 miles on the same battery power.

Operating Time Left Chart shows projected operating time left based on the battery bank voltage level and operating speed. This reflects the same kind of information as the previous chart, but the relationship is even more dramatic.

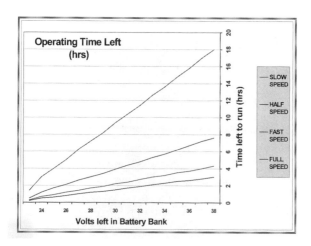

CONCLUSION:
Range goes up dramatically as speed goes down. If we run at full speed the range is about 9 miles on a bank, but at slow speed, we go almost 18 miles on the same battery power.

24

SHAKEDOWN CRUISE:
A REPORT CARD

We dreamed of a Chesapeake Bay vacation,
and we needed a shakedown cruise, but what could such contradictory
concepts possibly have in common?
Answer: Rose.

The idea sounded okay. When the restoration was done, we would take her on a shakedown cruise. Then we would fix the problems and do the final finishing. When *Rose* was perfect, we would take a vacation cruise as a reward for years of dedication. How could such a great plan not work?

Everything took longer than expected. The drive system was the major delay, but we also had deck leaks, plumbing, galley, stove, finishing, and other issues. The 2001 season passed as *Rose* made it only a few miles before something broke. Though we delayed repeatedly, we forgot to reset our June 2002 vacation. The closer we got to our vacation, the more we jammed in. In a moment of brilliance, we decided to finish the restoration and fix the problems on a working shakedown cruise, while pretending it was a vacation.

This meant that we would be carrying about a ton of parts and tools, a welcome stowage issue on a 25-foot boat already overloaded for a three-week trip. Is this what they mean when they say a plan came together? (Planning: C-)

Rose was wearing her best finery. Her brass was properly mounted with a mellowed patina. Her nameplates were just so, with two extra coats of varnish, and her fresh hull paint sported new striping and sheers. As expected when heading out in public, her batteries were fully charged and her belts were tightened, giving an extra spring to her motion. Her stained sails gave her a touch of character, trimmed by new lines and halyards in matching colors.

Rose is stable and comfortable, but we could hardly believe how much stuff she carried. Her heavy keel and hefty beam give her a degree of sure-footedness we didn't expect in a 25-foot boat, and she performed like a true lady even in abusive conditions. However, before we were free to roam the

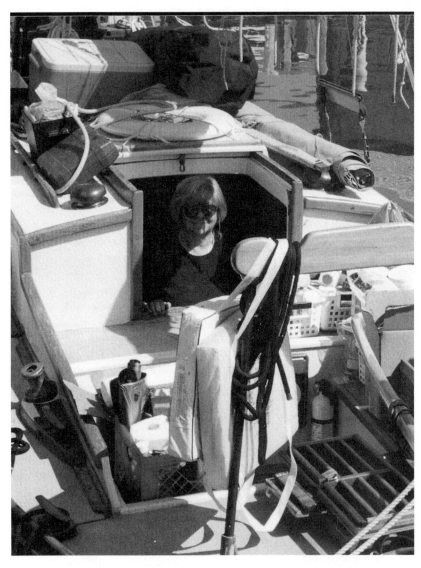

A dubious Cheryl asks, "And exactly how am I supposed to get all this stuff into the boat?" Incredibly, most of it fit and even seemed well organized, though a serious program to get rid of nonessentials helped.

Bay, *Rose* had to break the Curse of Turkey Point. She would not venture far from her friends at Bay Boat Works. Three times she tried to pass Turkey Point and failed. Now, she was ready. She was stronger, self-confident, and today was the day.

We motored down to marker #4 and raised sails to a so'westerly breeze. We dashed headlong into the Bay going South to Grove Point at the

Sassafras. Turning briskly in her first serious tack, she stuttered and faltered (it had been awhile), finally dragging herself onto a westerly tack. We had to learn to work with *Rose*: how high she points, how to tack, where lines go, how to tie things, and what doesn't fit. As Cheryl said in her diary, "We were learning. *Rose* would teach us."

Finding her wind, we trimmed sails and sped toward Mulberry Point. This process was repeated three times, and after a 14-mile sail, we slipped into Still Pond. The curse of Turkey Point had been broken. *Rose* was a free spirit again; ready to explore the world south of her new home.

Rose tolerated our ineptness. She feels like a small ship, and as the trip progressed, we gained more confidence. Sails and rig worked well considering their age and our lack of experience, and we were happy with how she handled off-wind. Jibing was simple and relatively foolproof, even for single-handed sailing, though retuning the rigging helped. Though some things were broken or repaired, we let her down more than she let us down. (Cockpit: A+)

There is little to compete with the subtle thrill of a sailing vessel on a perfect tack. The blended balance of aero-, hydro-, and physical dynamics can be felt and sensed more than calculated. The throb of the lines dims, as the pitch of the wind rises slightly, and the flap of the sails dies as the air flows smoothly around them. The hull stops splashing and thumping as water slips around the form. All seems in balance, Zen-like in its complexity and simplicity at the same time.

In few pursuits does the adage, "you'll know when it is right," make more sense. As the days slipped by, we came closer and closer to finding that magic point with *Rose*. Then, on Tuesday in the first week of June in the year of our Lord 2002, on the Chester River in Maryland, we found it and a grand time was had by all. (Sailing: B+)

Some problems were obvious. The knotmeter claimed we were doing 2 1/2 knots. No problem, I adjusted it to read higher. But I could not deny the truth; we were S-L-O-W. Facing reality, we had to make her go faster. (Speed: C+)

We ordered new sails but to raise a gaff-rigged sail, mast, and peak, halyards should move in unison, but ours did not. We'll fix that so the halyards synchronize when we rerig.

The line and handling layout from the cockpit worked out well, both while sailing and at anchor. The instrument panel was attractive and well positioned, but instruments were unreliable and inaccurate, particularly under power.

Dangling precariously from the forestay over the "widow-maker" in an energetic sea convinced me to build a platform on the bowsprit and handrails on the foredeck. Cheryl also wants to mount her swiveling cannon on it, but for less bellicose moments it will also hold hand-lines. (Foredeck: C+)

Later, we jammed the roller reefing and gaff boom and got beat up pretty bad. We made safe harbor after 30 scary minutes and promptly performed a serious cleaning and grease-job on the roller reefing and halyards, set up new reefing lines on the mainsail, and worked on some halyard rigging and twisting issues we discovered the hard way. (Rigging: D)

Fear also visited in fog as dense as any we had tried to navigate in. This should not be a concern, but I confess, in our rush to leave, the compass was not reading true. The unreliable depth sounder denied us good depth readings and the knotmeter-log randomly died, so dead reckoning was impossible.

The instruments' lack of performance placed us in potential danger, including grounding with the wind blowing us onto a sandbar. We had to get them working right away. (Instrumentation: F)

In total, we spent nine days fixing things, buying more stuff, and goofing off. We completed some projects, fixed rigging and operational problems, sorted out stowage issues, replaced a burned-out multimeter, and adjusted rigging and instruments. By halfway through the trip, almost everything was working, though there were a number of projects we will work on later.

In our first real-world test of the electric drive system, we motored up rivers, entered and left harbors, and handled bad traffic, channels, and anchoring. Several times we turned the motor on to assist the sails, pointing, and safety when winds were finicky or tides were heavy.

We are delighted with the quiet, easy-to-use, and nonpolluting system. We traveled 75 miles with power (28 percent of travel time) higher than we planned in our design assumptions (estimated motoring was 10 percent). It shows what estimates are worth compared to good records. (Range: B)

The motor drove us down the Miles River as we fought our way into St. Michaels against tide and winds. We ran at max power for half an hour to get past the worst spot. Minutes before our arrival, we began to lose power, gradually and predictably, so we switched to bank #2 to get in. (Power: C)

Motoring through Back Creek channel near Hart Island was worse. The slow speed (3-4 knots) is a problem in high traffic channels and areas with strong currents or headwinds. The drive system needs more speed (5-6 knots) to be 100 percent satisfactory. (Electric Drive overall: B)

Sailing comfort is critical, but comfort at anchor and harbor is important too. Here *Rose* proved to be a charmer and a refuge. *Rose* is comfortable with her 42-inch draft, wide decks, large hatches, and plentiful space. Her appearance also invites visitors and friends to stop by. The anchors are being replaced for better deck use and ease of handling. The radar reflector in the rigging is critical, since wood is invisible to radar.

The anchoring system is wrong. A small boat cannot stow two anchors on the deck; the space is too precious. We will switch to one midsized plow anchor with a chain on the bowsprit and a backup anchor. (Anchoring: C)

The cork decks work well, but the nonskid surface stains. We will put sealer with UV protection over the cork. (Decks B+)

The sound of a wooden boat is radically different. The lack of clanging halyards on the mast, the splash of waves against the hull, and mellow sounds in the cabin prove we are on a special boat. (Sound: A)

Just 15 feet long and 8 feet wide, *Rose*'s interior uses every inch of space. The table, ladder, and curtains move to set it up for different purposes and a touch of privacy. *Rose*'s galley is complete with sink, stove, ice chest, trash can, and lots of wood and brass. It supports meal preparation and works well. We will replace the hand pump for external water with an electric pump and add a utensil tray. (Galley: A+)

The companionway ladder and shelves separate the head from the galley, with the ice chest below. The ladder stows in the head to free up galley space while fixing meals. The shelves next to the ladder hold small items such as VHF radio, GPS, binoculars, camera, horn, and sunburn lotion. The main electrical panel with 120-VAC, 12-VDC, and 36-VDC controls is accessible with the ladder in place. The salon table is beautiful, but it is a bit large in the small cabin, and we want the leaves to open in dependently. The bulkhead between the settee and toilet area is too high for ease of movement.

The warmth and comfort of a wooden boat overcame small spaces with a traditional kind of coziness. The generous use of brass and warm wood finishes in the interior help a lot when stuck below in stormy weather. The folding salon table moves out of the settee and bunk area at night. The forward berth is large, even with the mast through the center, and getting in and out is eased by the brass handrail across the cabin edge. We are pleased with the layout and we will finish the interior during the winter. (Cabin: A-)

There are many minor items that determine the livability of a vessel. It may be a hook in the right place, or a nice shelf that is perfectly positioned. All these items are crucial to successful sailing and living on board. We feel that *Rose* is in good shape in this category of livability.

The Kerosene stove worked after another rebuild. The biggest problem is trying to get started because an unwieldy propane torch preheats the burners. Despite our best efforts, we could not use more than one burner at a time. Then it blew another gasket and died again. Our patience was tested enough, and we will do something major with it. (Stove: D)

High on the list are irritating leaks over the berth. The forward hatch also leaks and collects condensation to drip down. Sealing, better ventilation, and gutters will help, but a canvas cover will prevent water from getting to the hatch, which may be smart. The main hatch is strong and waterproof, but it needs a latch to keep it from sliding accidentally. Despite the bronze mushroom vents and eight portholes, the airflow through the cabin is an issue and we will look at more ventilation and better screens and hatch boards. (Ventilation: B-)

We were surprised to see many restored or rebuilt wooden vessels; it was reassuring that we were not the only eccentrics willing to save these beasts.

The scariest event was in Chestertown, when Cheryl found another boat in need of love and attention. I have forgotten what was said, but I remember the glazed look in her eyes, and I got us out of there right away. (Overall grade for the boat: B+)

We started and ended in Northeast and visited 14 Chesapeake Bay harbors. *Rose* kept us comfortable and safe for 22 days and carried us about 300 miles, and on 13 days, we averaged about 19 miles per day. I decided to enjoy the trip despite the pace. My idle brain calculated the speed Columbus made to find the New World; 3,100 miles divided by 91 days was 34 miles per day, or about 1.5 knots, average speed. They did great things at about half the speed we were traveling.

Our best lesson was speed (or lack thereof). The appeal of a slower pace, in keeping with the events around us, grew each day. We had a great trip but averaged only 3 knots. At such speeds, it is not the *getting-to* that counts, but the *going-to*. Oddly, we had time to explore since we were not busy going fast. I wonder just how much we miss in our push for more speed? *Rose* taught me that if I go slow enough, I can see a lot more (of the beauty and wonder) of the Bay.

Strangely, when the trip was over, it was my impression that *Rose* looked better than when we started. The changes, nicks, and scratches gave her more of a comfortable look. No longer was she just another pretty face. *Rose* was a proven and hardened traveler, ready for the worst and enjoying the best. It went okay for a shakedown cruise.

Only *Rose* could combine a shakedown cruise with a vacation and get away with it.

We celebrated our 35th anniversary on the cruise. Despite the rigors of a 22-day trip and sharing a space the size of a bathroom, Cheryl agreed to keep me around a bit longer. We learned that only great friends can explore the Bay at 3 knots.

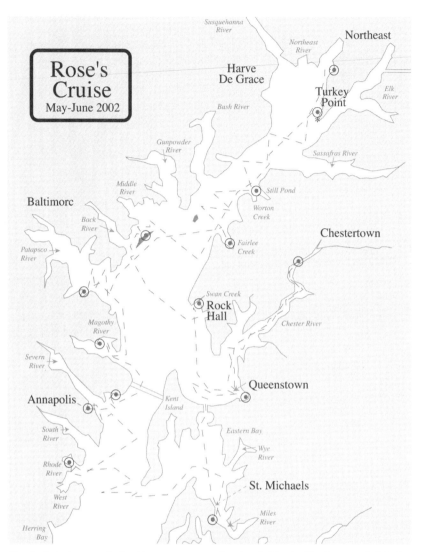

Rose's shakedown cruise/maiden voyage started and ended in the Northeast and visited
14 Chesapeake Bay harbors almost 300 miles in 22 days. After five years of work, the
cruise was the proof of a successful plan and execution. It was also an opportunity to
refine the design and implementation.

25

MY FATHER'S HANDS

I remember my father's hands. They were tough and callused from years of manual labor building creations of wood, metal, brick, and mortar. There were ugly splits where calluses were broken by strain, with scars and wounds attesting to his accomplishments. He made things. Things that had not existed an hour, a day, a week, or a month before. Things of all shapes and descriptions.

Those hands were aged as if life somehow slipped from his flesh into the object, carrying a bit of him with it. I admired those hands, knowing the beauty and functionality he created had started there.

Both my brothers work with their hands, and our forebears worked with their hands. The trait apparently skipped me, leaving me "tool-impaired" from my earliest years. Anything I tried to create came out amateurish, to be patched with putty and encased in thick paint, or covered with another object, or dumped in the trash, often unfinished.

I even humorously nicknamed myself a DOFW (a Destroyer of Fine Wood) after a teenaged debacle with a bookcase. It was not lack of desire, for I dreamed of great things, but the abyss between what my mind saw and the final product was too formidable. I was the studious one, the "absent-minded professor." Eventually I stopped trying, doing only what was needed as an auto-, boat-, or homeowner, assuring myself, "Well, it works!"

I recently said goodbye to my father. Knowing the story of his time on this planet, I couldn't help but think that he had a tough life. Looking at his hands that last time, I reassured myself that my life was better than his, because my hands did not show the pain and damage his had suffered.

My hands were soft and uncallused, indicative of someone who works with books and computers. Such was the state of my hands when we adopted *Rose*. My hands would soon change, as would I.

When I went to a mill-shop for wood, a discovery process began that continued throughout the project, and maybe for the rest of my life. A foraging expedition evolved into a near-religious experience. I began to think about wood; my ruminations were inspired by the smell, feel, and look of something unique and appealing.

As the mill-man explained the options, I realized that wood is the ultimate building material. It comes in an incredible variety to fill any need, and no two pieces are the same.

I was looking for white oak to replace timbers and ribs in the hull. I learned that this was different than other types of oak. White oak is great for rigid components but also nice for pieces that must flex, such as ribs. It was all very confusing.

White cedar is different than other cedars. It is light and strong, but not as resistant to rot as the red, oily cedars. Its open cells can be damaged easily, but it is perfect for a boat, if it does not get damaged. It sands easily and paints up to look beautiful.

Mahogany comes in many flavors. It is great for carving and finishing. Teak is often the wood of choice, though it is heavy and resistant to paint. The yellow pine of the keel is most interesting, wood that hardly rots, yet it is strong and flexible.

I've heard somewhere that hiding within each piece of wood is its preferred destiny of what it would become if only we could see. It seems that man is the questionable element in this godly pursuit.

I discovered that an amateur can analyze what wood has to offer, but it is hard to interpret its subtle signals, and even harder yet to help it to its final destiny with my meager skills.

Once I got it home, I discovered another quirk of wood. It seems content to just lie there until it feels threatened by a power tool. Then it reveals its ability to move, trying to get away. I tried talking and rubbing it gently before starting, but my ministrations seemed to have little effect once the power tool howled. Clamps and jigs became the first step in every job no matter how minor.

Most frustrating was trying to get things to fit. I cut carefully, measured and remeasured, sanded true, clamped, glued, and screwed. However, when the clamps came off, there were no square corners, straight lines, or properly fitting edges.

I became a bit paranoid, sneaking to the bench while glue was drying and peering suspiciously at the *objet d'art*. Perhaps I felt a gremlin was sabotaging my work, something like the sock monster that hides in clothes dryers.

I remembered the apparent ease of my father when he picked up a hunk of wood or metal and transformed it into something. One would think that a degree in math would help, but for me, even measuring things is a challenge. It seems that any hunk of wood, once cut, will not fit; it may be too long or too short, have the wrong angle, not be flat, be too flat, or not be square.

As I marshaled the courage to rebuild *Rose*, I rationalized that most of my experience was with houses and other squarish objects. I entertained the idea that since nothing in a boat is straight, I would have better luck, hypothesizing that maybe crookedness could become a virtue.

Unfortunately, that theory was wiped out by the first roar of the saw. Cautiously, I tried again and again, and not only could I not match the drawings, but the wood had shrunk smaller than the drawing!

In frustration, I kept trimming, determined to make something out of the hunk of wood. I resolved the disparity between the drawing and the work, the fiction and the fact, by trashing the drawing. To finish, I worked by eye and by feel alone.

Soon a shape appeared. Some sanding, a little trim here, a little trim there, and something began to emerge to my surprise. I found myself holding the pieces up before my eyes, gazing along the periphery, estimating where and how much to cut, then trimming and holding it up for inspection again.

The idea was revolutionary, but I tried it to carve the nameplates into graceful curves. It worked well and with less frustration and greater satisfaction.

I chuckled that to an unknowing observer, I must have looked a bit like my father at work years before. I remember him succeeding even as my mother called out measurements as "11 and 3 little bits" or "26 and 2 big bits."

An odd thing, I began viewing the boat and its components in a new fashion, as if it were alive. I no longer thought a piece of wood was damaged, now I thought of it as injured; it wasn't gouged, it had a wound; it wasn't rotten, it was diseased. A kind of delicacy crept in, as new thinking took root.

The fit and finish showed the effects, as I invested time in details, coming closer to perfection in the final product than I ever imagined. I felt empathy for woodworkers of old and their pride and commitment that I had not appreciated before. I sensed a strong tie to my Norse ancestors and the living spirits of the wood that protected their vessels.

I began to see an error in our modern way of thinking, the idea that time is money. Instead, I invested whatever time it took, and the value of time was measured only by the results. This unfamiliar concept fits an older way of thinking, the way that leads to amazing art and great accomplishments.

Four years later, Rose was finally in the water, though a lot was left to be done. I had worked harder than any time in my life, and I was tired as I turned off tools and lights and prepared to close down the shop one evening.

I straightened my aching back a bit in pride as I confirmed that dozens of components were ready to be installed. I double-checked batteries, and motor and electrical controls set for the next day's work.

I reviewed pieces that would come together to create the interior. On and on the lists went, through half a yellow pad. I stood for a moment on the step and surveyed the workshop, filled with many failures and many successes.

I gave a part of me to all of them and I hurt in so many places I could not count them all. I turned off the light after one more glance, and then climbed the steps, tired, but with a feeling of accomplishment.

At the kitchen sink, I washed my hands, picking out splinters and trimming calluses with an X-Acto knife that permanently resided next to the soap and the Intensive Care lotion. I removed the worn Band-Aids and dried carefully to not break open any wounds. From the first aid drawer, (now next to the kitchen sink), I put on new dressings.

The left index finger tip (removed by the planer) was healing, and in a few more weeks it would be a scar. On the same finger, above the joint, there was a mark where the wrench slipped. On the middle finger of the left hand, there was an irritating cyst from an earlier injury. Two more minor dinks on the left hand. The right hand was okay, only two small Band-Aids, and I was done.

In the dim light, I had a sudden vision, a feeling of déjà vu. Maybe it was fatigue, but as I looked at my abused hands, for just a moment, my mind slipped back 50 years, and I thought I was looking at my father's hands.

Shock, disbelief, and rejection of the heretical notion flushed over me. The arrogance of the idea!

As I dumped the debris in the trash, the feeling hung in the air like a phantasm. I opened the basement door and turned on the light, unsure of why I was retracing my steps. I walked back down the stairs and stood there looking at the enormity of the tasks now completed. I glanced over the tools discovered, the mounds of sawdust and chunks of wood, the finished objects, the failures, the close saves, the proud masterpieces.

I slowly realized my father's hands were not the hands of knowledge, skill, and talent that I had seen them as, but rather the hands of experience, work, and courage. It was the experience of many failures, the work of many successes, and the courage to fail, to find the success that was needed.

I smiled more comfortably, held my hands and fingers up to frame my handiwork, and said to myself proudly, "OK, my father's hands."

It was ironic. I begrudgingly started working on *Rose* to save her, and she taught me things I hardly realized I should know. I owe a debt of gratitude to *Rose* and my father; maybe wood boats are more about people than I imagined.

26

OUTTAKES

I will get this confession out: If I had invested all my time productively, I could have finished *Rose* in three years instead of six, at half the cost. I spent time figuring out what to do, buying wrong stuff, doing wrong things, redoing them, then doing something different. If Hollywood can do it, then so can do-it-yourselfers. I call these stories, "Outtakes."

At my age, I am convinced that more character-building opportunities are unnecessary, but these stories suggest that God disagrees. The money and work they represented was critical to the success of *Rose*. Such exercises helped develop skills, reveal design weaknesses, or show us what would not work. Our standards of safety, design, taste, and appearance were raised and seasoned by these experiences. In a sense, our best year was when we created the greatest number of outtakes.

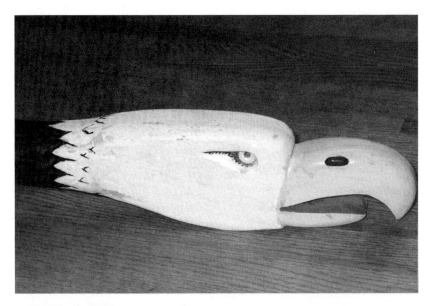

A Bird-Headed Tiller
A tiller had a bizarre visage which I refinished to resemble a cross between the
Philadelphia Eagles and the United States Postal Service logos. It took an
unconscionable amount of work, and is as unique a tiller as I have ever laid eyes upon.
However, we could not let it on the beautiful boat we had created, so I chopped the head
off as a memento.

A Walt Disney Toilet

A friend gave us a marine toilet that stopped working long before most of us started using one. It was resurrected into something resembling a movie prop from Disney's campy treatment of 20,000 Leagues Under the Sea, EXCEPT... a hairline crack showed up, that tried to sink the boat. It was replaced with a new $150 toilet with only 2-hours installation.

Star Trek Motor Flange

I manufactured this mounting flange from a chunk of aluminum for our golf cart motor, with cooling fins, handles, adjustment holes and alignment ports. With its yellow fan and spring loaded adjusters, it even worked! Scotty of Star Trek would have loved it! The motor died and was replaced and this chunk of engineering sits on a shelf... too pretty to throw out!

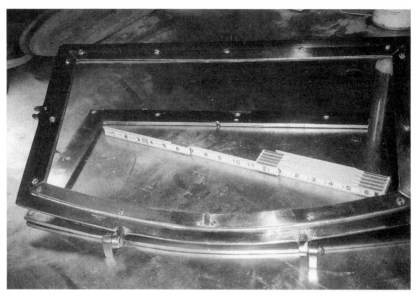

A Big Brass Hatch

I bought a big porthole / window thing with solid brass frames and curved top and heavy glass and decided it SHOULD be useful SOMEWHERE! It is too large for the boat, had no waterproofing and is too heavy to install in anything that moves.

FUNGI

I tried to create a rose with carving chisels. After hours of work, I congratulated myself for creating something artistic in wood for the first time! With its curves, delicate bevels and meticulously crafted surfaces, my rose looked suspiciously like <u>fungus</u> on a tree! I shared my artwork with my spouse, assuring her that we could rename the boat FUNGI!

Teak Handrails and Bronze Stanchions

I lay guilt for this on my friend Al. While he was finishing the interior, I tumbled across a set of teak and bronze handrails for a 50-foot motor yacht. I mentioned them, noting the lack of safety lines on the boat. He insisted I get them since "it is such a great deal I can't NOT do it!" They are twice as big as our 25 footer, so they still sit in the basement.

A Mast Ladder
My (*no longer buns of steel*) refuse to spring to the masthead anytime the vessel demands it, so I created a rope ladder. The theory sounded good, but as I climbed, the ladder settled with much creaking and groaning. The strain of my immense presence caused it to stretch into an elongated structure with steps too far apart to go further! I hid the evidence.

Two New Black Anchors

These new anchors were painted black to match the boat's rigging and chains. They look great but they use too much foredeck space and were tough to handle on and off the boat. We replaced then with a large plow anchor hanging off the bowsprit and a mushroom anchor for gunkholing. Anybody need two new black anchors in good condition?

INDEX

Hazard, George, 10, 15, 19, 21
Heat generation, 142
Heat gun, 39, 40, 93
Heavy weather locker, 121
Heel, 84
Heel indicator, 74
Hell Gate (New York City), 114
Helmsman, 74
Hindenburg, 148
Holly plywood, 106
Hoops, 138
Horns, 89
Hull, 4, 9, 11, 12, 14, 15, 18, 23, 32, 35, 49, 57, 82,
    83, 90, 92, 100, 101, 133, 134, 137, 155, 159, 161,
    162, 175, 181, 183, 188
Hull planks, 5
Hull speed, 177
Hull structure, 48
Ice chest, 81, 82, 85, 86, 103, 183
Ingots, 135
Inner Harbor, 9
Intensive Care lotion, 190
Interior, 119, 136, 137, 183
Interior trim, 105
Internal combustion, 58
Jib, 70, 160, 166, 167
Jib sheets, 73
Jibing, 181
Jigs, 24, 86, 100, 188
Johnson & Johnson, 123
Jolly Roger, 17
Keel, 6, 12, 13, 20, 135, 159, 161, 179, 188
Keel beam, 10
Keel crossbeams, 19
Kerosene stove, 183
Kerosene system, 99
Kerosene tank, 102
Key switch, 76
Kiln-dried wood, 53
King planks, 20, 47, 49, 51, 52
KiwiProp, 175
Knotmeter, 75
Ladder, 125, 152
Laminated wood tiller, 76
Lazarette, 62, 75, 92, 113, 116, 117, 141, 144,
    171, 172
Lazarette hatch, 53, 76, 77, 90, 145
Lazarette hatch, 90
Lazy jacks, 160, 168
LifeCaulk, 54
Linseed oil stain/sealer, 54
Lloyd's registry certificate, 32
Lock pin, 142
Locker design, 100
Lockers, 72, 74, 114, 116
London, England, 68
Long Island Sound, 3, 115
Low deck hatch, 113
Low quarter berth, 115
Mahogany, 19, 33, 43, 52, 53, 67, 75, 111, 116, 188
Mahogany ceilings, 33
Mahogany hatch, 27
Mahogany ladder, 152
Mahogany main hatch, 76
Maiden voyage, 119, 185
Main boom, 40, 78, 155
Main bulkhead, 32
Main halyard, 44, 157, 160
Main hatch, 54, 103, 110, 113, 116, 121, 183
Mainsail, 44, 155, 157, 161, 163–167
Mainsheet, 73

Manual bilge pump, 73
Marine motor, 169
Marine plywood, 32, 86, 90, 100, 109, 122, 150
Mast, 39, 40, 49, 120, 155, 162, 166, 167, 181, 183
Mast boot, 136, 138
Mast deck collar, 133
Mast ladder, 197
Mast step, 5, 10, 14, 15, 17, 19, 90, 161
Mast stepping, 138, 156
Masthead, 157
Masthead block, 160
Masthead flag halyard, 70
Masthead light, 136, 152
Mechanical systems, 121
Miles River (Chesapeake Bay), 182
Minigalley, 82
Miter saw, 108
Motor, 135, 136
Motor and drive system, 176
Motor mounts, 62
Motor space, 114
Mulberry Point, 181
Multimeter, 182
Mushroom vents, 183
Nameplate, 66, 68–70, 137, 179
Navigation charts, 122
Navigation station, 74
New England, 6, 47, 81
New York City, 114
Nonskid sand, 109
Oak ribs, 19
Oceanus Tanbark, 168
One-way check valves, 139
Operating Range•Left Chart, 178
Operating Time Left Chart, 178
Oscillating sander, 150
Outhaul, 166
Paint sprayer, 31
Pam spray, 166, 167
Paper tape, 108
Peak halyard, 155, 157, 160
Pennsylvania, 18
Pequeño, 3
Philadelphia Eagles, 71, 192
Piano hinges, 107
Pinder, Master Sergeant (Ret.) Frank, 129,
    130, 131
Plank hull, 147
Plank-and-caulk hull, 55
Plastic tanks, 93
Plow anchor, 151
Plumbing, 92, 100, 101, 121, 123, 179
Plywood decks, 148
Plywood, 107, 108, 148
Poop deck, 72, 73
Portholes, 183
Potentioneter, 174
Power drain, 142
Power panels, 121
Power plugs, 75, 89
Power system, 92
Primary solenoid, 173
Prop, 115, 142, 144, 168, 175, 176
Prop shaft, 143, 169
Propane torch, 100
Propeller, 60, 61, 62, 162
Propeller shaft, 60
Prop-shaft stuffing box, 61
Propulsion system controls, 74
Pull-down line, 166
PVC lines, 73